10

chocolate

Published in 2009 by Murdoch Books Pty Limited.
www.murdochbooks.com.au

Murdoch Books Australia
Pier 8/9, 23 Hickson Road
Millers Point NSW 2000
Phone: + 61 (0) 2 8220 2000
Fax: + 61 (0) 2 8220 2558

Murdoch Books UK Limited
Erico House, 6th Floor
93–99 Upper Richmond Road
Putney, London SW15 2TG
Phone: + 44 (0) 20 8785 5995
Fax: + 44 (0) 20 8785 5985

Chief Executive: Juliet Rogers
Publishing Director: Kay Scarlett
Publisher: Jane Lawson
Commissioning Editor: Lynn Lewis

Concept & Design: Sarah Odgers
Art Direction: Heather Menzies
Editor: Kate Fitzgerald
Photographer: Jared Fowler
Stylist: Cherise Koch
Production: Alexandra Gonzalez
Food preparation: Alan Wilson
Introduction text: Leanne Kitchen
Recipes developed by the Murdoch Books Test Kitchen

National Library of Australia Cataloguing-in-Publication Data
Kitchen Classics Chocolate. Includes index.
ISBN 9781741963076 (pbk.)
Series: Kitchen Classics
Subjects: Cookery, (Chocolate) Cake, Desserts.
Other Authors/Contributors: Price, Jane
Dewy Number: 641.6374
A catalogue record is available from the British Library.

Colour reproduction by Splitting Image Colour Studio, Melbourne, Australia.
Printed by 1010 Printing International Limited in 2009. PRINTED IN CHINA.

IMPORTANT: Those who might be at risk from the effects of salmonella poisoning (the elderly, pregnant woman, young children and those suffering from immune deficiency diseases) should consult their doctor with any concerns about eating raw eggs.
CONVERSION GUIDE: You may find cooking times vary depending on the oven you are using. For fan-forced ovens, as a general rule, set the oven temperature to 20°C (35°F) lower than indicated in the recipe.

chocolate

THE CHOCOLATE RECIPES YOU MUST HAVE

SERIES EDITOR JANE PRICE

MURDOCH BOOKS

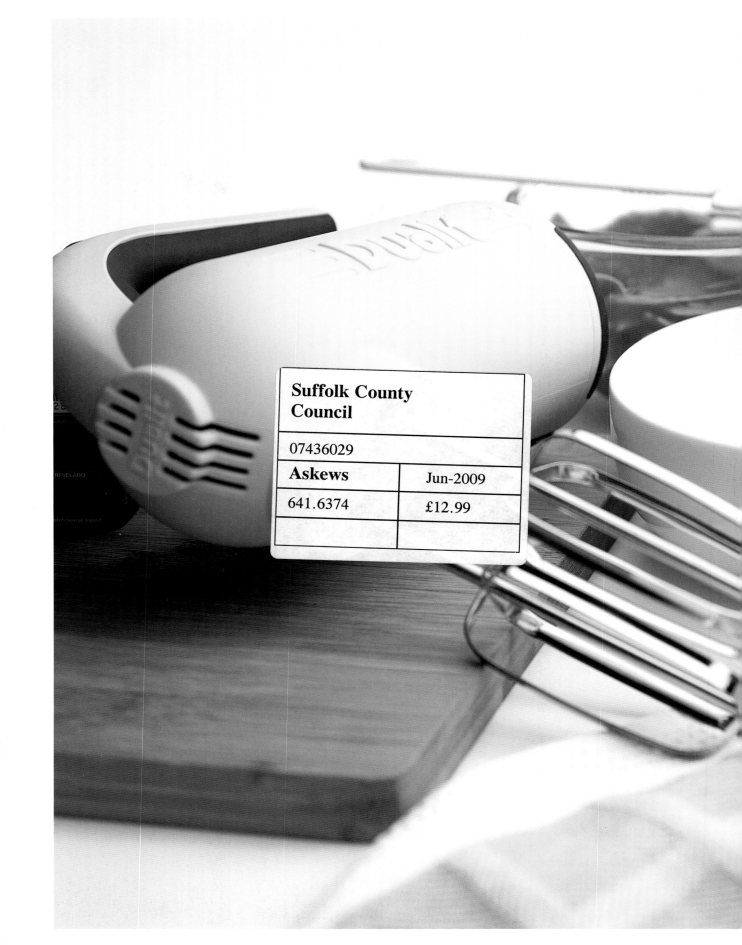

Suffolk County Council	
07436029	
Askews	Jun-2009
641.6374	£12.99

CONTENTS

CHOCOLATE KISSES   6

A PIECE OF CAKE   8

TEA TIME TREATS   50

COLD AND CREAMY   90

HOT AND SAUCY   130

CRISPY CRUNCHY   170

MEMORABLE MORSELS   212

INDEX   250

CHOCOLATE KISSES

Chocolate is irresistible no matter what form you eat it in, whether it's neat squares straight from the packet, or savoured in the myriad chocolate cakes, cookies or desserts that can be made from it. Eating and cooking with chocolate can be dangerously addictive.

As all chocolate lovers know, there are three main types: white, milk and dark. Within these categories, one finds products of varying quality; when purchasing chocolate (even for cooking), it is important to be armed with a little knowledge. Chocolate should contain 'cocoa solids' and 'cocoa butter'; the solids lend the characteristic brown colour while the butter gives chocolate a delicious 'snap' when broken and that lush mouth-feel. Because cocoa butter is so expensive, inferior chocolates skimp on it, using cheap vegetable fat as a substitute. The amount of combined cocoa solids and cocoa butter (called 'cocoa mass') chocolate contains should be displayed as a percentage on the packaging.

Bittersweet is the strongest tasting of all chocolates, it is not terribly sweet and is mainly used in baking. This dark chocolate generally has a cocoa mass content of 63 to 72 per cent. Semi-sweet chocolate is also dark, and has a cocoa mass content of 52 to 62 per cent. Semi-sweet chocolate is good for both cooking and eating straight. Milk chocolate contains milk powder and more sugar than dark; good-quality milk chocolate will contain 36 to 46 per cent cocoa mass. White chocolate is pale as it contains no cocoa solids. Good-quality white chocolate gets its ivory colour and silky smoothness from cocoa butter (a quality one will contain around 28 per cent), although cheap white chocolate (to be avoided at all costs) contains vegetable fat instead.

If this all sounds overwhelming, it's truly not. To identify quality chocolate, all you need do is read the labels. A word of caution though: once you've tasted quality chocolate, there's absolutely no going back.

A PIECE OF CAKE

ANGEL FOOD CAKE WITH CHOCOLATE SAUCE

125 g (4½ oz/1 cup) plain (all-purpose) flour
230 g (8 oz/1 cup) caster (superfine) sugar
10 egg whites, at room temperature
1 teaspoon cream of tartar
½ teaspoon vanilla extract

CHOCOLATE SAUCE
250 g (9 oz/1²/₃ cups) chopped
dark chocolate
185 ml (6 fl oz/³/₄ cup) cream
50 g (1³/₄ oz) chopped unsalted butter

SERVES 8

Preheat the oven to 180°C (350°F/Gas 4). Have an ungreased angel cake tin ready. Sift the flour and half the sugar four times into a large bowl. Set aside.

Beat the egg whites, cream of tartar and ¼ teaspoon salt with electric beaters until soft peaks form. Gradually add the remaining sugar and beat until thick and glossy. Add the vanilla.

Sift half the flour and sugar mixture over the meringue and gently fold in with a metal spoon. Do the same with the rest of the flour and sugar. Spoon into the tin and bake for 45 minutes, or until a skewer comes out clean when poked into the centre of the cake. Gently loosen around the side of the cake with a spatula, then turn the cake out onto a wire rack to cool completely.

To make the chocolate sauce, put the chocolate, cream and butter in a saucepan. Stir over low heat until the chocolate has melted and the mixture is smooth. Drizzle over the cake and serve.

PREPARATION TIME: 30 MINUTES   COOKING TIME: 50 MINUTES

FLOURLESS CHOCOLATE CAKE

500 g (1 lb 2 oz/3⅓ cups) chopped dark chocolate
6 eggs, at room temperature
2 tablespoons Frangelico or brandy
165 g (5¾ oz/1½ cups) ground hazelnuts
250 ml (9 fl oz/1 cup) cream, whipped
icing (confectioners') sugar and cream, to serve

SERVES 10

Preheat the oven to 150°C (300°F/Gas 2). Grease a 20 cm (8 inch) round cake tin and line the base with baking paper.

Put the chocolate in a heatproof bowl. Half fill a saucepan with water, bring to the boil, then remove from the heat and sit the bowl over the pan (don't let the bowl touch the water or the chocolate will get too hot and seize). Stir occasionally until the chocolate melts.

Put the eggs in a heatproof bowl and add the Frangelico. Put the bowl over a pan of barely simmering water — don't let it touch the water. Beat the eggs with electric beaters on high speed for 7 minutes, or until light and foamy. Remove from the heat.

Using a metal spoon, quickly and lightly fold the chocolate and ground hazelnuts into the eggs. Fold in the whipped cream and pour the mixture into the cake tin. Put the cake tin in a roasting tin and pour enough boiling water into the roasting tin to come halfway up the side of the cake tin. Bake for 1 hour, or until a skewer comes out clean when poked into the centre of the cake. Remove the cake tin from the water bath and cool to room temperature. Cover with plastic wrap and refrigerate overnight.

Turn out the cake onto a plate, remove the paper and cut into slices. Dust with icing sugar and serve with cream.

PREPARATION TIME: 20 MINUTES   COOKING TIME: 1 HOUR

WHITE CHOCOLATE AND ALMOND CAKES

140 g (5 oz/1 cup) chopped
white chocolate
85 g (3 oz) chopped unsalted butter
125 ml (4 fl oz/1/2 cup) milk
115 g (4 oz/1/2 cup) caster (superfine) sugar
1 egg, at room temperature
115 g (4 oz/3/4 cup) self-raising flour, sifted
55 g (2 oz/1/2 cup) ground almonds
12 raspberries and icing (confectioners')
sugar, to serve

WHITE CHOCOLATE GANACHE
400 g (15 1/2 oz) finely chopped
white chocolate
170 ml (5 1/2 fl oz/2/3 cup) cream

MAKES 12

Preheat the oven to 190°C (375°F/Gas 5). Line a 12-hole muffin tray with paper cases.

Mix together the chocolate, butter and milk in a saucepan. Stir over low heat until melted and smooth. Transfer to a bowl and set aside to cool a little. Whisk in the sugar and egg.

Mix together the flour and ground almonds, then add to the bowl and mix well. Spoon into the muffin holes and bake for 20 minutes, or until a skewer comes out clean when poked into the centre of a cake. Leave in the tray for 5 minutes before transferring to a wire rack to cool.

Meanwhile, to make the white chocolate ganache, place the chocolate in a heatproof bowl. Heat the cream in a saucepan until it is almost simmering. Add to the chocolate and leave for 1 minute, then stir until smooth. Cool in the fridge, stirring occasionally, until the ganache has a thick, spreadable consistency.

To serve, spread the ganache over the cakes. Top each one with a raspberry and dust with a little icing sugar.

PREPARATION TIME: 30 MINUTES   COOKING TIME: 30 MINUTES

MARBLE CAKE

1 vanilla bean or 1 teaspoon vanilla extract
185 g (6½ oz) chopped unsalted butter, softened
30 g (8 oz/1 cup) caster (superfine) sugar
3 eggs, at room temperature
280 g (10 oz/2¼ cups) self-raising flour
185 ml (6 fl oz/¾ cup) milk
2 tablespoons unsweetened cocoa powder
1½ tablespoons warm milk

SERVES 6

Preheat the oven to 200°C (400°F/Gas 6). Lightly grease a 25 x 11 x 7.5 cm (10 x 4¼ x 3 inch) loaf (bar) tin and line the base with baking paper.

Split the vanilla bean down the middle and scrape out the seeds. Put the seeds (or vanilla extract) in a bowl with the butter and sugar and, using electric beaters, cream the mixture until pale and fluffy. Add the eggs one at a time, beating well after each addition. Sift the flour, then fold it into the creamed mixture alternately with the milk until they are combined. Put half the mixture into another bowl.

Mix the cocoa and warm milk until smooth, then add to one of the bowls and mix well. Spoon the plain mixture and chocolate mixture into the tin in alternating spoonfuls. Use a metal skewer to gently cut through the mixture a few times to create a marbled effect. Bake for 50-60 minutes, or until a skewer comes out clean when poked into the centre of the cake. Leave in the tin for 5 minutes before turning out onto a wire rack to cool. Cut into slices and serve.

PREPARATION TIME: 20 MINUTES   COOKING TIME: 1 HOUR

RICH FUDGE AND MARSHMALLOW CRUST CAKE

125 g (4½ oz/1 cup) plain (all-purpose) flour
30 g (1 oz/¼ cup) self-raising flour
30 g (1 oz/¼ cup) unsweetened cocoa powder
1 teaspoon bicarbonate of soda (baking soda)
115g (4 oz/½ cup) caster (superfine) sugar
60 g (2¼ oz/⅓ cup) soft brown sugar
1 egg, at room temperature
1 teaspoon vanilla extract
60 g (2¼ oz) unsalted butter, melted
125 ml (4 fl oz/½ cup) milk
125 g (4¼ oz) white mini marshmallows
icing (confectioners') sugar, to dust

SERVES 8–10

Preheat the oven to 180°C (350°F/Gas 4). Brush a 23 cm (9 inch) round cake tin with melted butter or oil. Line the base with baking paper.

Sift the flours, cocoa and bicarbonate of soda into a large bowl. Add the sugars and make a well in the centre. Combine the egg, vanilla, butter and milk and pour into the well. Stir until smooth, then stir in the marshmallows.

Pour into the tin and smooth the surface. Bake for 40-45 minutes, or until a skewer comes out clean when poked into the centre of the cake.

Leave in the tin for 25 minutes before turning out onto a wire rack to cool completely. Dust with icing sugar before serving.

PREPARATION TIME: 20 MINUTES   COOKING TIME: 45 MINUTES

DATE CHOCOLATE TORTE

100 g (3½ oz/¾ cup) slivered almonds
150 g (5½ oz/1 cup) chopped dark chocolate
120 g (4¼ oz/⅔ cup) pitted dried dates
3 egg whites, at room temperature
115 g (4 oz/½ cup) caster (superfine) sugar
125 ml (4 fl oz/½ cup) cream, for whipping
2 teaspoons caster (superfine) sugar, extra
grated dark chocolate, to serve

SERVES 6

Preheat the oven to 180°C (350°F/Gas 4). Grease a 22 cm (8½ inch) spring-form cake tin and line with foil. Finely chop the almonds and chocolate in a food processor. Finely chop the dates.

Beat the egg whites with electric beaters until soft peaks form. Slowly add the sugar and continue beating until the sugar dissolves. Fold in the almond and chocolate mixture, then the dates. Spoon into the tin and smooth the surface. Bake for 30–35 minutes, or until a skewer comes out clean when poked into the centre of the torte. Leave in the tin to cool a little before turning out onto a serving plate.

To serve, whip the cream and extra sugar until soft peaks form. Spread over the cake and sprinkle with the grated chocolate.

PREPARATION TIME: 20 MINUTES   COOKING TIME: 35 MINUTES

CHOCOLATE WALNUT RING

210 g (7½ oz/1¾ cups) self-raising flour
1 teaspoon bicarbonate of soda (baking soda)
60 g (2¼ oz/½ cup) unsweetened cocoa powder
170 g (6 oz/¾ cup) caster (superfine) sugar
45 g (1½ oz/¼ cup) soft brown sugar
1 teaspoon vanilla extract
2 eggs, at room temperature
250 ml (9 fl oz/1 cup) buttermilk
125 ml (4 fl oz/½ cup) milk
60 g (2¼ oz) unsalted butter, melted
40 g (1½ oz/⅓ cup) chopped walnuts
icing (confectioners') sugar, to dust

CHOCOLATE SAUCE
100 g (3½ oz/⅔ cup) chopped dark chocolate
80 ml (2½ fl oz/⅓ cup) cream

SERVES 6–8

Preheat the oven to 180°C (350°F/Gas 4). Brush a 23 cm (9 inch) fluted ring tin with melted butter or oil and line the tin with baking paper.

Sift the flour, bicarbonate of soda and cocoa into a large bowl and add the sugars. Make a well in the centre. Mix together the vanilla, eggs, buttermilk, milk and butter and pour into the well. Using electric beaters, beat on high speed for 5 minutes, or until smooth and increased in volume. Fold in the walnuts.

Pour into the tin and smooth the surface. Bake for 35 minutes, or until a skewer comes out clean when poked into the centre of the cake. Leave in the tin for 10 minutes before turning out onto a wire rack to cool.

To make the chocolate sauce, mix together the chocolate and cream in a saucepan over low heat. Stir until melted and smooth. Remove from the heat and leave to cool to room temperature. Pour the sauce over the cake and dust with icing sugar.

PREPARATION TIME: 35 MINUTES   COOKING TIME: 35 MINUTES

Date chocolate torte

CHOCOLATE COFFEE MOUSSE MERINGUE CAKE

6 eggs, at room temperature, separated
375 g (13 oz/1²/₃ cups) caster (superfine) sugar
2½ tablespoons unsweetened cocoa powder, plus extra to dust
1 tablespoon instant coffee granules
200 g (7 oz) dark chocolate
600 ml (21 fl oz) cream, whipped

SERVES 10–12

Preheat the oven to 150°C (300°F/Gas 2). Cut four pieces of baking paper large enough to line four baking trays. On three of the pieces of paper, mark a 22 cm (8½ inch) circle. On the remaining piece, draw straight lines, 3 cm (1¼ inches) apart. Line the baking trays with the paper.

Beat the egg whites until soft peaks form. Gradually add the sugar, beating well after each addition. Beat for 5-10 minutes, until thick and glossy and all the sugar has dissolved. Gently fold the sifted cocoa into the meringue.

Divide the meringue into four portions. Spread three portions over each of the marked circles. Put the remaining meringue in a piping (icing) bag fitted with a 1 cm (½ inch) plain piping nozzle. Pipe lines about 8 cm (3¼ inches) long over the marked lines. Bake for 45 minutes, or until pale and crisp. Check the meringue strips occasionally to prevent overcooking. Turn off the oven and cool in the oven with the door ajar.

Put the chocolate in a heatproof bowl. Half fill a saucepan with water, bring to the boil, then remove from the heat and sit the bowl over the pan (don't let the bowl touch the water or the chocolate will get too hot and seize). Stir occasionally until the chocolate melts.

Dissolve the coffee granules in 1 tablespoon water. Put the melted chocolate in a bowl, whisk in the egg yolks and the coffee mixture, and beat until smooth. Fold in the whipped cream and mix the whole lot together. Refrigerate until the mousse is cold and thick.

To assemble, place one meringue disc on a plate and spread with one-third of the mousse. Top with another disc and spread with half the remaining mousse. Repeat with the remaining disc and mousse. Run a knife around the edge of the meringue cake to spread the mousse evenly over the edge. Cut or break the meringue strips into short pieces and pile them on top of the cake, pressing them into the mousse. Dust with cocoa powder and refrigerate until firm.

PREPARATION TIME: 20 MINUTES +   COOKING TIME: 50 MINUTES

CHOCOLATE MUFFINS

310 g (11 oz/2½ cups) self-raising flour

40 g (1½ oz/⅓ cup) unsweetened cocoa powder

½ teaspoon bicarbonate of soda (baking soda)

145 g (5 oz/⅔ cup) caster (superfine) sugar

375 ml (13 fl oz/1½ cups) buttermilk

2 eggs, at room temperature

160 g (5½ oz) unsalted butter, melted and cooled

MAKES 12

Preheat the oven to 200°C (400°F/Gas 6). Lightly grease a 12-hole muffin tray. Sift the flour, cocoa powder and bicarbonate of soda into a bowl and add the sugar. Make a well in the centre.

In a jug, whisk together the buttermilk and eggs and pour into the well. Gently fold in the butter with a metal spoon. Do not overmix — the mixture should still be lumpy.

Fill each hole about three-quarters full. Bake for 20–25 minutes, or until a skewer comes out clean when poked into the centre of a muffin. Leave the muffins in the tray for 5 minutes before transferring to a wire rack to cool. Serve warm or at room temperature.

PREPARATION TIME: 15 MINUTES   COOKING TIME: 25 MINUTES

CHOCOLATE BANANA CAKE

3 ripe bananas, mashed

170 g (6 oz/¾ cup) caster (superfine) sugar

185 g (6½ oz/1½ cups) self-raising flour

2 eggs, at room temperature, lightly beaten

60 ml (2 fl oz/¼ cup) light olive oil

60 ml (2 fl oz/¼ cup) milk

100 g (3½ oz/¾ cup) grated dark chocolate

90 g (3¼ oz/¾ cup) chopped walnuts

SERVES 6–8

Preheat the oven to 180°C (350°F/Gas 4). Lightly grease a 20 x 10 cm (8 x 4 inch) loaf (bar) tin and line the base with baking paper.

Mix together the mashed banana and sugar. Add the sifted flour, eggs, oil and milk. Stir gently for 30 seconds with a wooden spoon. Fold in the chocolate and walnuts.

Pour into the tin and bake for 55 minutes, or until a skewer comes out clean when poked into the centre of the cake. Leave in the tin for 5 minutes before turning out onto a wire rack. Serve warm with cream.

PREPARATION TIME: 15 MINUTES   COOKING TIME: 55 MINUTES

Chocolate muffins

BLACK FOREST CAKE

185 g (6½ oz) unsalted butter, softened
170 g (6 oz/¾ cup) caster
(superfine) sugar
3 eggs, at room temperature,
lightly beaten
1 teaspoon vanilla extract
210 g (7½ oz/1⅔ cups) self-raising flour
40 g (1½ oz/⅓ cup) plain
(all-purpose) flour
90 g (3 oz/¾ cup) unsweetened
cocoa powder
1 tablespoon instant coffee granules
½ teaspoon bicarbonate of soda
(baking soda)
125 ml (4 fl oz/½ cup) buttermilk
80 ml (2½ fl oz/⅓ cup) milk
310 ml (10¾ fl oz/1¼ cups) cream,
whipped
425 g (15 oz) tin pitted cherries, drained
chocolate curls, for decoration

CHOCOLATE TOPPING
300 g (10½ oz/2 cups) chopped
dark chocolate
375 g (13 oz) unsalted butter,
softened

SERVES 8–10

Preheat the oven to 180°C (350°F/Gas 4). Grease a 23 cm (9 inch) round cake tin and line the base and side with baking paper.

Cream the butter and sugar with electric beaters until light and fluffy. Add the eggs gradually, beating thoroughly after each addition. Add the vanilla and beat until well combined.

Using a metal spoon, fold in the sifted flours, cocoa, coffee and bicarbonate of soda alternately with the combined buttermilk and milk. Stir until almost smooth.

Pour into the tin and smooth the surface. Bake for 40–50 minutes, or until a skewer comes out clean when poked into the centre of the cake. Leave in the tin for 20 minutes before turning out onto a wire rack to cool.

To make the chocolate topping, put the chocolate in a heatproof bowl. Half fill a saucepan with water and bring to the boil. Sit the bowl over the pan but don't let the bowl touch the water or the chocolate will get too hot and seize. Allow to stand, stirring occasionally, until the chocolate has melted. Beat the butter until light and creamy. Add the chocolate, beating for 1 minute, or until the mixture is glossy and smooth.

Turn the cake upside down and cut into three layers horizontally. Place the first layer on a serving plate. Spread evenly with half the whipped cream, then top with half the cherries. Continue layering with the remaining cake, cream and cherries, ending with the cake on the top cut side down. Spread the chocolate topping over the top and side using a flat-bladed knife. Using a piping (icing) bag and the remaining topping, pipe swirls around the cake rim. Decorate with chocolate curls.

PREPARATION TIME: 1 HOUR   COOKING TIME: 1 HOUR

DEVIL'S FOOD CAKE WITH STRAWBERRY CREAM

280 g (10 oz/2¼ cups) self-raising flour
85 g (3 oz/⅔ cup) unsweetened
cocoa powder
345 g (12 oz/1½ cups) caster
(superfine) sugar
3 eggs, at room temperature,
lightly beaten
150 g (5½ oz) unsalted butter, softened
icing (confectioners') sugar, to dust

CHOCOLATE CURLS
100 g (3½ oz/⅔ cup) chopped
milk chocolate
90 g (3¼ oz/⅔ cup) chopped
white chocolate

GANACHE
225 g (8 oz/1½ cups) chopped
dark chocolate
70 g (2½ oz) unsalted butter

STRAWBERRY CREAM
250 ml (9 fl oz/1 cup) whipping cream
2 tablespoons icing (confectioners') sugar
300 g (10½ oz/2 cups) strawberries
1 teaspoon vanilla extract
4 tablespoons strawberry jam
2 tablespoons orange liqueur

SERVES 8–10

Preheat the oven to 180°C (350°F/Gas 4). Grease a 24 cm (9½ inch) round cake tin and line the base with baking paper. Sift the flour and cocoa into a large bowl. Add the sugar, eggs, butter and 250 ml (9 fl oz/1 cup) water. Using electric beaters, beat on low speed for 1 minute. Increase the speed to high and beat for a further 4 minutes. Pour into the tin. Bake for about 55 minutes, or until a skewer comes out clean when poked into the centre of the cake. Leave in the tin for 20 minutes before turning out onto a wire rack to cool completely.

To make the chocolate curls, put the milk and white chocolate in separate heatproof bowls. Half fill a saucepan with water and bring to the boil. Individually, sit the bowls over the saucepan. Allow to stand, stirring occasionally until the chocolate has melted. Spread the melted chocolate separately in thin layers onto a flat surface. Allow to set. Using a knife at a 45-degree angle, form long, thin curls by pushing the knife through the chocolate away from you. Refrigerate the curls until needed.

To make the ganache, put the chocolate and butter in a heatproof bowl. Half fill a saucepan with water and bring to the boil. Sit the bowl over the pan, but don't let the bowl touch the water. Allow to stand, stirring occasionally until the chocolate has melted. Set aside to cool slightly.

To make the strawberry cream, beat the cream and icing sugar together until thick. Refrigerate until needed. Set aside 8 whole strawberries, and hull and chop the remainder. Just before using, fold the chopped strawberries and vanilla through the cream. Mix together the jam and liqueur. Cut the cake in half horizontally. Place the bottom half on a serving plate and spread evenly with the jam, then the strawberry cream. Top with the other cake half. Spread the ganache smoothly over the top of the cake. Arrange the milk and white chocolate curls and the strawberries decoratively over the cake. To serve, dust the cake with icing sugar and cut into wedges.

PREPARATION TIME: 1 HOUR   COOKING TIME: 1 HOUR

WALNUT AND CHOCOLATE PLUM TORTE

200 g (7 oz/2 cups) walnuts
200 g (7 oz/1⅓ cups) chopped
dark chocolate
2 teaspoons instant coffee granules
100 g (3½ oz/heaped ¾ cup)
cornflour (cornstarch)
200 g (7 oz) unsalted butter, softened
185 g (6½ oz/1 cup) raw caster
(superfine) sugar
4 eggs, at room temperature, separated
2 teaspoons coffee liqueur
450 g (1 lb) small firm plums (angelina
or sugar plums are ideal) or 800 g
(1 lb 12 oz) medium to large plums,
halved and stoned
2 tablespoons dark brown sugar
20 g (¾ oz) unsalted butter, extra
vanilla ice cream or whipped cream,
to serve

SERVES 8–10

Preheat the oven to 170°C (325°F/Gas 3). Grease a 25 cm (10 inch) spring-form cake tin and line the base with baking paper.

In a food processor, grind the walnuts and chocolate until finely processed. Add the coffee granules and cornflour and process briefly.

Cream the butter and sugar with electric beaters until pale. Add the egg yolks, one at a time, alternately with some of the walnut mixture, beating well after each addition. Stir in the liqueur.

Whisk the egg whites until soft peaks form. Fold a large spoonful into the walnut mixture, then gently fold the rest of the egg white through. Spoon into the tin and smooth the surface. Bake for 30 minutes.

Remove from the oven and arrange the plums, cut side up, on top of the cake. Scatter the brown sugar over the plums and dot the extra butter over the sugar. Return the torte to the oven and bake for another 40 minutes, or until a skewer comes out clean when poked into the centre.

Remove the torte from the oven and cool for 1 minute, then carefully run a knife around the edge to prevent any toffee sticking to the tin. Leave in the tin for 15 minutes before turning out onto a wire rack. Serve warm in slices, accompanied with softened vanilla ice cream or whipped cream.

PREPARATION TIME: 30 MINUTES   COOKING TIME: 1 HOUR 10 MINUTES

CHOCOLATE AND AMARETTI REFRIGERATOR CAKE

250 g (9 oz/1²/₃ cups) chopped
dark chocolate
1 tablespoon instant coffee granules
250 g (9 oz) unsalted butter, softened
185 g (6¹/₂ oz/1 cup) raw caster
(superfine) sugar
1 tablespoon unsweetened cocoa powder
3 eggs, at room temperature, separated
50 g (1³/₄ oz/¹/₂ cup) flaked almonds,
toasted
50 g (1³/₄ oz/¹/₄ cup) glacé (candied)
cherries, halved
300 g (10¹/₂ oz) amaretti biscuits
2 tablespoons cognac

SERVES 8

Line a 22 cm (8¹/₂ inch) spring-form cake tin with plastic wrap.

Put the chocolate in a heatproof bowl. Half fill a saucepan with water and bring to the boil. Sit the bowl over the pan, but don't let the bowl touch the water or the chocolate will get too hot and seize. Stir frequently until the chocolate has melted, slowly adding in the coffee, then leave to cool.

Beat the butter and sugar with electric beaters until light and fluffy, then sift in the cocoa and beat well. Add the egg yolks one at a time, beating well after each addition. Fold in the melted chocolate.

In a separate bowl, whisk the egg whites until stiff peaks form. Using a metal spoon, gently fold into the chocolate mixture. Add the almonds and glacé cherries and fold through.

Put a tightly fitting single layer of amaretti on the base of the tin, flat side down. Drizzle a little cognac over them. Spread half the chocolate on top, then cover with another layer of amaretti. Drizzle with cognac, cover with the rest of the chocolate mixture and put a final tight layer of amaretti on top, flat side down. Knock the tin on the work surface a couple of times to pack the cake layers down. Cover the top with plastic wrap and refrigerate overnight.

Remove the cake from the tin. It will be sufficiently set to enable you to upturn it onto one hand, peel off the plastic wrap and set it down on a serving plate, right way up. Cut into wedges to serve.

PREPARATION TIME: 30 MINUTES   COOKING TIME: 5 MINUTES

YULE LOG

60 g (2¼ oz/½ cup) plain (all-purpose) flour
2 tablespoons unsweetened cocoa powder
3 eggs, at room temperature
80 g (2¾ oz/⅓ cup) caster (superfine) sugar, plus extra to sprinkle
50 g (1¾ oz) unsalted butter, melted and cooled

FILLING
125 g (4½ oz) white chocolate, chopped
125 ml (4 fl oz/½ cup) cream
50 g (1¾ oz) finely chopped toasted hazelnuts

TOPPING
125 g (4½ oz) chopped dark chocolate
125 ml (4 fl oz/½ cup) cream
icing (confectioners') sugar, to dust

SERVES 8

Preheat the oven to 180°C (350°F/Gas 4). Brush a 30 x 35 cm (12 x 14 inch) Swiss roll tin (jelly roll tin) with oil or melted butter and line the base and sides with baking paper. Sift the flour and cocoa together twice. Using electric beaters, beat the eggs and sugar for 5 minutes, or until light, fluffy and thick.

Sift the flour and cocoa mixture over the eggs and pour the butter around the edge of the bowl. Using a metal spoon, fold in the flour and butter. Take care not to overmix or you will lose too much volume.

Spread into the tin and bake for 12 minutes, or until a skewer comes out clean when poked into the centre of the cake. Sprinkle the extra caster sugar over a clean tea towel. Turn the sponge out onto the tea towel close to one end. Roll up the sponge and tea towel together lengthways and leave to cool.

To make the filling, put the white chocolate in a small heatproof bowl. Bring a saucepan of water to the boil, then remove from the heat. Add the cream to the chocolate and sit the bowl over the pan of water, making sure the bowl does not touch the water, until the chocolate is soft. Stir until smooth. Do this for the dark chocolate and cream for the topping. Leave the white chocolate mixture until it has cooled to room temperature and is the consistency of cream. Leave the dark chocolate mixture until it cools and is spreadable.

Beat the white chocolate mixture with electric beaters until soft peaks form, but do not overmix or it will curdle. Unroll the sponge, remove the tea towel and spread the sponge with the filling, finishing 2 cm (¾ inch) from the end. Sprinkle with the hazelnuts. Reroll the sponge and trim the ends. Cut off one end on the diagonal and place it alongside the log to create a branch.

Place the yule log on a serving plate and spread the dark chocolate topping all over it. Run a fork along the length of the roll to give a 'bark' effect. Just before serving, decorate with fresh unsprayed green leaves, such as geranium leaves, and dust with icing sugar.

PREPARATION TIME: 40 MINUTES   COOKING TIME: 20 MINUTES

CHOCOLATE CHESTNUT ROULADE

60 g (2¼ oz) dark chocolate, chopped
4 eggs, at room temperature
115 g (4 oz/½ cup) caster (superfine) sugar
100 g (3½ oz) tinned sweetened chestnut purée
60 g (2¼ oz/½ cup) self-raising flour, sifted
unsweetened cocoa powder, for dusting

CHESTNUT CREAM
150 g (5½ oz) tinned sweetened chestnut purée
300 ml (10½ fl oz) thick (double/heavy) cream
1 tablespoon dark rum

SERVES 6–8

Preheat the oven to 180°C (350°F/Gas 4). Lightly grease a 25 x 30 cm (10 x 12 inch) Swiss roll tin (jelly roll tin) and line the base with baking paper.

Put the chocolate in a heatproof bowl. Half fill a saucepan with water, bring to the boil, then remove from the heat and sit the bowl over the pan (don't let the bowl touch the water or the chocolate will get too hot and seize). Stir occasionally until the chocolate melts. Allow to cool.

Whisk the eggs and sugar for 5 minutes, or until pale and very thick. Beat in the chestnut purée and melted chocolate, then fold in the flour and 2 tablespoons hot water. Gently pour into the tin and bake for 20 minutes, or until a skewer comes out clean when poked into the centre of the cake. (Be careful not to overcook the cake or it will crack when it's rolled.)

Put a tea towel on the work surface, cover with a piece of baking paper and lightly dust with cocoa. Turn the cake out onto the paper, then carefully remove the baking paper from the base of the cake. Trim the edges to neaten. Using the tea towel as a guide, carefully roll the cake up from the long side, rolling the paper inside the roll. Put the rolled cake on a wire rack and leave to cool for 10 minutes, then carefully unroll and cool completely.

To make the chestnut cream, beat the chesnut purée, cream and rum until just thick. Spread the cake with the chestnut cream, then carefully reroll, using the paper to guide you. Place the roulade, seam side down, on a serving plate and dust the top generously with cocoa powder.

PREPARATION TIME: 30 MINUTES COOKING TIME: 25 MINUTES

SACHER TORTE

125 g (4½ oz/1 cup) plain (all-purpose) flour
30 g (1 oz/¼ cup) unsweetened cocoa powder
230 g (8 oz/1 cup) caster (superfine) sugar
100 g (3½ oz) unsalted butter
80 g (2¾ oz/¼ cup) strawberry jam
4 eggs, at room temperature, separated

GANACHE TOPPING
170 ml (5½ fl oz/⅔ cup) cream
80 g (2¾ oz/⅓ cup) caster (superfine) sugar
200 g (6½ oz/1⅓ cups) chopped dark chocolate

SERVES 8–10

Preheat the oven to 180°C (350°F/Gas 4). Lightly grease a 20 cm (8 inch) round cake tin and line with baking paper.

Sift the flour and cocoa into a bowl and make a well. Combine the sugar, butter and half the jam in a saucepan over low heat. Stir until the butter has melted and the sugar has dissolved, then pour into the well along with the lightly beaten egg yolks and mix well.

Beat the egg whites with electric beaters until soft peaks form. Stir a third of the egg white into the cake mixture, then fold in the rest in two batches. Pour into the tin and smooth the surface. Bake for 40–45 minutes, or until a skewer comes out clean when poked into the centre of the cake. Leave in the tin for 15 minutes before turning out onto a wire rack to cool.

To make the ganache topping, stir the cream, sugar and chocolate in a saucepan over low heat until melted and smooth.

Trim the top of the cake so that it is flat, then turn it upside down on a wire rack over a tray. Melt the remaining jam and brush it over the cake. Pour most of the topping over the cake and tap the tray to flatten the surface of the topping. Place the remaining mixture in a piping bag and pipe 'Sacher' on top of the cake.

PREPARATION TIME: 40 MINUTES   COOKING TIME: 1 HOUR

BUTTERFLY CHOCOLATE CAKES

60 g (2¼ oz) unsalted butter, softened
80 g (2¾ oz/⅓ cup firmly packed) soft brown sugar
½ teaspoon vanilla extract
1 egg, at room temperature
60 g (2½ oz/¼ cup) self-raising flour
30 g (1 oz/¼ cup) unsweetened cocoa powder
2 tablespoons milk
60 g (2 oz/¼ cup) thick (double/heavy) cream
80 g (2¾ oz/¼ cup) raspberry jam
icing (confectioners') sugar, to dust

MAKES 24

Preheat the oven to 180°C (350°F/Gas 4). Line two 12-hole muffin trays with paper cases.

Beat the butter, sugar and vanilla until pale and creamy. Add the egg and beat well. Sift together the flour and cocoa. Add half the flour mixture to the butter and whisk gently, then add the milk and mix together. Add the rest of the flour and mix well.

Divide evenly among the paper cases. Bake for 15–20 minutes, or until a skewer comes out clean when poked into the centre of a cake. Transfer to a wire rack to cool.

Cut a shallow round from the centre of each cake, then cut the round in half. Fill the centres of the cakes with a little cream and some raspberry jam. Position the two cake wedges on the cream, pressing them down very gently to resemble butterfly wings. Dust with sifted icing sugar.

PREPARATION TIME: 20 MINUTES   COOKING TIME: 20 MINUTES

CHOCOLATE RUM AND RAISIN CAKE

2 tablespoons dark rum
40 g (1½ oz/¼ cup) chopped raisins
220 g (7¾ oz/1⅓ cups) self-raising flour
40 g (1½ oz/⅓ cup) plain (all-purpose) flour
40 g (1½ oz/⅓ cup) unsweetened cocoa powder
170 g (6 oz/¾ cup) caster (superfine) sugar
55 g (2 oz/¼ cup) raw (demerara) sugar
200 g (7 oz) unsalted butter
1 tablespoon golden syrup
100 g (3½ oz/⅔ cup) chopped dark chocolate
2 eggs, at room temperature, lightly beaten
icing (confectioners') sugar and unsweetened cocoa powder, to serve
cream, to serve

Preheat the oven to 150°C (300°F/Gas 2). Brush a 20 cm (8 inch) round cake tin with melted butter or oil. Line the base and side of the tin with baking paper.

Combine 60 ml (2 fl oz/¼ cup) water, the rum and raisins in a small bowl and set aside. In a separate bowl, sift the flours and cocoa and make a well in the centre.

Combine the sugars, butter, golden syrup and chocolate in a saucepan. Stir over low heat until the butter and chocolate have melted and the sugar has dissolved, then remove from the heat. Stir in the raisin and rum mixture.

Using a metal spoon, fold the butter and chocolate mixture into the well. Add the eggs and mix well until smooth. Pour into the tin and smooth the surface. Bake for 1 hour, or until a skewer comes out clean when poked into the centre of the cake. Leave in the tin for 1 hour before turning out onto a wire rack. Dust with sifted cocoa and icing sugar. Cut the cake into wedges and serve warm with cream.

SERVES 8–10   PREPARATION TIME: 20 MINUTES   COOKING TIME: 1 HOUR 5 MINUTES

41

ORANGE, LEMON AND WHITE CHOCOLATE GATEAU

125 g (4½ oz/1 cup) plain (all-purpose) flour

4 eggs, at room temperature

145 g (5 oz/⅔ cup) caster (superfine) sugar

60 g (2 oz) unsalted butter, melted and cooled

FILLING

2 tablespoons cornflour (cornstarch)

80 ml (2½ fl oz/⅓ cup) lemon juice

80 ml (2½ fl oz/⅓ cup) orange juice

1 teaspoon grated lemon zest

1 teaspoon grated orange zest

80 g (2¾ oz/⅓ cup) caster (superfine) sugar

2 egg yolks, at room temperature

20 g (¾ oz) unsalted butter

TOPPING

200 g (7 oz) chopped white chocolate

125 ml (4 fl oz/½ cup) cream

60 g (2¼ oz) unsalted butter

white chocolate curls and candied citrus zest, to decorate

SERVES 8–10

Preheat the oven to 180°C (350°F/Gas 4). Grease two 20 cm (8 inch) round cake tins and line the bases and sides with baking paper.

Sift the flour onto a sheet of baking paper. Beat the eggs and sugar until thick, pale and increased in volume. Using a metal spoon, fold in the flour in two batches, quickly and lightly. Add the melted butter with the second batch, discarding any white sediment in the butter. Spread into the tins and bake for 20 minutes, or until a skewer comes out clean when poked into the centre of a cake. Leave in the tins for 2 minutes before turning out onto a wire rack to cool.

To make the filling, blend the cornflour with 1 tablespoon water to make a paste. Place 3 tablespoons water, the juice, zest and sugar in a saucepan and stir over medium heat, without boiling, until the sugar has dissolved. Add the cornflour paste and bring to the boil. Stir for 1 minute. Remove from the heat, add the egg yolks and butter and stir well. Transfer to a bowl, cover the surface with plastic wrap and cool completely.

To make the topping, place the chocolate, cream and butter in a saucepan and stir over low heat until the chocolate and butter have melted. Transfer to a bowl, cover with plastic wrap and allow to cool completely. Do not refrigerate. Once cool, beat until fluffy.

Using a serrated knife, cut the cakes in half horizontally. Place one cake layer on a serving plate and spread the filling evenly over it. Continue layering the cake and filling, ending with a cake layer on top. Spread the top and sides of the cake with the topping. Decorate with white chocolate curls and candied lemon rind.

PREPARATION TIME: 1 HOUR   COOKING TIME: 35 MINUTES

GINGER CAKES WITH CHOCOLATE CENTRES

100 g (3½ oz) unsalted butter, softened
125 g (4½ oz/⅔ cup) soft brown sugar
115 g (4 oz/⅓ cup) treacle or dark corn syrup
2 eggs, at room temperature
125 g (4½ oz/1 cup) self-raising flour
85 g (3 oz/⅔ cup) plain (all-purpose) flour
2 teaspoons ground cinnamon
1 tablespoon ground ginger
60 ml (2 fl oz/¼ cup) buttermilk

CHOCOLATE GANACHE
100 g (3½ oz/⅓ cup) chopped dark chocolate
60 ml (2 fl oz/¼ cup) cream
1 tablespoon finely chopped glacé ginger

MAKES 12

Preheat the oven to 180°C (350°F/Gas 4). Line a 12-hole muffin tray with paper cases.

To make the chocolate ganache, put the chocolate in a small heatproof bowl. Heat the cream until almost boiling, then pour over the chocolate and stir until it has melted and the mixture is smooth. Stir in the glacé ginger. Cool to room temperature, then chill in the refrigerator until firm. Divide the mixture into 12 equal portions and roll each into a ball. Freeze until required.

Using electric beaters, cream the butter, sugar and treacle until pale and fluffy. Add the eggs one at a time, beating well after each addition. Transfer to a large bowl. Sift the flours and spices into the mixture, then fold into the butter mixture alternately with the buttermilk.

Divide three-quarters of the mixture among the paper cases. Top each with a ball of frozen ganache, then cover the ganache with the rest of the mixture. Bake for 25–30 minutes, or until the cakes are deep golden (the cakes cannot be tested with a skewer as the centres will be molten). Leave to cool for 5 minutes. Remove the paper cases and serve warm.

PREPARATION TIME: 15 MINUTES +   COOKING TIME: 35 MINUTES

CHOCOLATE BEETROOT CAKES

cooking oil spray

125 g (4½ oz/1 cup) plain (all-purpose) flour

40 g (1½ oz/⅓ cup) unsweetened cocoa powder

1½ teaspoons bicarbonate of soda (baking soda)

½ teaspoon baking powder

1 teaspoon mixed spice

230 g (8 oz/1 cup firmly packed) soft brown sugar

75 g (2½ oz/¾ cup) walnut halves, chopped

170 ml (5½ fl oz/⅔ cup) canola or vegetable oil

2 eggs, at room temperature

225 g (8 oz) beetroot, finely shredded

CHOCOLATE DRIZZLE ICING

195 g (6¾ oz/1¼ cups) icing (confectioners') sugar

30 g (1 oz/¼ cup) unsweetened cocoa powder

MAKES 8

Preheat the oven to 180°C (350°F/Gas 4). Spray 8 ramekins with oil to grease and place on a large baking tray.

Sift together the flour, cocoa, bicarbonate of soda, baking powder and mixed spice. Stir in the sugar and walnuts, then make a well in the centre.

Whisk together the vegetable oil and eggs. Add the beetroot and stir. Pour into the well and, using a large metal spoon, fold them together. Divide the mixture among the ramekins and smooth the surfaces.

Bake for 20 minutes, or until a skewer comes out clean when poked into the centre of a cake. Leave the cakes in the ramekins for 5 minutes before turning out onto a wire rack to cool.

To make the chocolate drizzle icing, sift together the icing sugar and cocoa. Add 60 ml (2 fl oz/¼ cup) boiling water and mix until smooth. Drizzle the cakes with the icing. Set aside for 30 minutes, or until the icing is set. Serve with thick cream or ice cream.

PREPARATION TIME: 20 MINUTES   COOKING TIME: 20 MINUTES

RICH CHOCOLATE AND WHISKY MUD CAKE WITH SUGARED VIOLETS

250 g (9 oz) unsalted butter, cubed
200 g (7 oz/1⅓ cups) chopped dark chocolate
375 g (13 oz/1⅔ cups) caster (superfine) sugar
125 ml (4 fl oz/½ cup) whisky
1 tablespoon instant coffee granules
185 g (6½ oz/1½ cups) plain (all-purpose) flour
60 g (2¼ oz/½ cup) self-raising flour
40 g (1½ oz/⅓ cup) unsweetened cocoa powder
2 eggs, at room temperature, lightly beaten

CHOCOLATE GLAZE
80 ml (2½ fl oz/⅓ cup) cream
90 g (3¼ oz/scant ⅔ cup) chopped dark chocolate

sugared violets, to decorate (optional; see Note)
silver cachous, to decorate

SERVES 8–10

Preheat the oven to 160°C (315°F/Gas 2–3). Grease a 20 cm (8 inch) square tin and line the base and sides with baking paper.

Put the butter, chocolate, sugar and whisky in a saucepan. Dissolve the coffee granules in 125 ml (4 fl oz/½ cup) hot water and add to the mixture. Stir over low heat until melted and smooth.

Sift the flours and cocoa into a large bowl, then pour in the butter mixture and whisk together. Whisk in the eggs and pour into the tin.

Bake for about 1 hour 15 minutes, or until a skewer comes out clean when poked into the centre of the cake. Pour the extra whisky over the cake. Leave in the tin for 20 minutes before turning out onto a wire rack, placed over a baking tray, to cool.

To make the chocolate glaze, put the cream in a small saucepan and bring just to the boil. Remove from the heat and add the chocolate. Stir until melted and smooth. Set aside to cool and thicken a little. Spread the glaze over the cake, allowing it to drizzle over the sides. Leave the glaze to set. Decorate with the sugared violets and silver cachous.

PREPARATION TIME: 40 MINUTES   COOKING TIME: 1 HOUR 25 MINUTES

NOTE: To make the sugared violets, use a small, clean artist's paintbrush to coat 16 fresh unsprayed violets with a thin layer of lightly beaten egg white. Sprinkle evenly with caster sugar. Stand the violets on a wire rack and leave to dry. When dry, store in an airtight container between layers of tissue. The violets are edible.

TEA TIME TREATS

CHOCOLATE ECLAIRS

125 g (4½ oz) unsalted butter
125 g (4½ oz/1 cup) plain (all-purpose)
flour, sifted
4 eggs, at room temperature,
lightly beaten
300 ml (10 fl oz) cream, whipped
150 g (5½ oz/1 cup) chopped
dark chocolate

MAKES 18

Preheat the oven to 210°C (415°F/Gas 6-7). Grease two baking trays. Combine the butter and 250 ml (9 fl oz/1 cup) water in a saucepan. Stir over medium heat until the butter melts. Increase the heat, bring to the boil, then remove from the heat.

Add the flour to the saucepan and quickly beat into the butter mixture with a wooden spoon. Return to the heat and continue beating until the mixture leaves the side of the pan and forms a ball. Transfer to a large bowl and cool slightly. Beat the mixture to release any remaining heat. Gradually add the egg, about 3 teaspoons at a time. Beat well after each addition until all the egg has been added and the mixture is glossy (a wooden spoon should stand upright). It will be too runny if the egg is added too quickly. If this happens, beat for several more minutes, or until thickened.

Spoon into a piping (icing) bag fitted with a 1.5 cm (⅝ inch) plain nozzle. Sprinkle the baking trays lightly with water. Pipe 15 cm (6 inch) lengths onto the trays, leaving room for expansion. Bake for 10–15 minutes, then reduce the heat to 180°C (350°F/Gas 4) and bake for another 15 minutes, or until golden and firm. Cool on a wire rack. Split each éclair, and remove any uncooked dough. Fill the éclairs with cream.

Put the chocolate in a heatproof bowl. Half fill a saucepan with water, bring to the boil, then remove the pan from the heat. Sit the bowl over the pan, making sure the bowl doesn't touch the water as the chocolate will get too hot and seize. Allow to stand, stirring occasionally, until the chocolate has melted. Spread over the top of each éclair.

PREPARATION TIME: 20 MINUTES   COOKING TIME: 40 MINUTES

BLACK AND WHITE CHOCOLATE TART

PASTRY

90 g (3¼ oz) unsalted butter,
at room temperature
55 g (2 oz/¼ cup) caster (superfine) sugar
1 egg, at room temperature, lightly beaten
185 g (6½ oz/1½ cups) plain
(all-purpose) flour
30 g (1 oz/¼ cup) self-raising flour
1 tablespoon unsweetened cocoa powder

FILLING

2 teaspoons powdered gelatine
200 ml (7 fl oz) milk
115 g (4 oz/½ cup) caster (superfine) sugar
80 g (2¾ oz/½ cup) chopped
white chocolate
4 egg yolks, at room temperature,
lightly beaten
250 ml (9 fl oz/1 cup) cream, whipped to
soft peaks

CHOCOLATE GLAZE

60 ml (2 fl oz/¼ cup) cream
80 g (2¾ oz/½ cup) chopped
dark chocolate
10 g (¼ oz) unsalted butter
2 teaspoons liquid glucose

SERVES 12

Preheat the oven to 190°C (375°F/Gas 5). Lightly grease the base and side of a 21 cm (8¼ inch) spring-form cake tin and line the base with baking paper.

To make the pastry, beat the butter with electric beaters until smooth and fluffy. Beat in the sugar and egg. Sift in the combined flours and cocoa and stir until the dough comes together. Knead briefly on a lightly floured surface until smooth. Flatten into a disc, cover with plastic wrap, and refrigerate for 30 minutes. Roll out the pastry between two sheets of baking paper until about 8 mm (3/8 inch) thick, and trim to fit the base of the tin. Ease the pastry into the tin, removing the paper, and lightly prick with a fork. Bake for 15 minutes, or until the pastry is slightly firm to the touch. Set aside to cool.

To make the filling, combine the gelatine and 2 tablespoons water in a small bowl and set aside for 2 minutes for the gelatine to sponge and swell. In a saucepan, bring the milk, sugar and white chocolate to a simmer. Stir until the sugar has dissolved and the chocolate has melted. Whisk the egg yolks into the warm chocolate mixture. Stir over medium heat until it lightly coats the back of a spoon. Add the sponged gelatine and stir until dissolved. Over a bowl of ice, beat until the mixture is cold, then fold in the cream. Pour over the pastry and refrigerate overnight, or until set.

To make the glaze, put the cream, dark chocolate, butter and glucose in a saucepan and stir over medium heat until smooth. Cool until thickened. Remove the tart from the tin and place on a serving plate. Spoon the glaze over the top of the tart, allowing it to drip down the side. Set aside at room temperature for 1 hour, or until the glaze is set.

PREPARATION TIME: 1 HOUR +   COOKING TIME: 25 MINUTES

CHOCOLATE FUDGE PECAN PIE

PASTRY
150 g (5½ oz/1¼ cups) plain
(all-purpose) flour
2 tablespoons unsweetened cocoa
powder
2 tablespoons soft brown sugar
100 g (3½ oz) unsalted butter, chilled
and cubed

200 g (7 oz/2 cups) pecan nuts,
roughly chopped
100 g (3½ oz/²/₃ cup) chopped
dark chocolate
95 g (3¼ oz/½ cup) soft brown sugar
170 ml (5½ fl oz/²/₃ cup) light or dark
corn syrup
3 eggs, at room temperature,
lightly beaten
2 teaspoons vanilla extract

SERVES 6

Preheat the oven to 180°C (350°F/Gas 4). Grease a 23 x 18 x 3 cm (9 x 7 x 1¼ inch) pie dish.

To make the pastry, sift the flour, cocoa and sugar into a bowl and rub in the butter with your fingertips until the mixture resembles fine breadcrumbs. Make a well and add 2–3 tablespoons iced water and mix with a knife, adding more water if necessary.

Lift the dough onto a sheet of baking paper. Press into a disc, cover with plastic wrap and refrigerate for 20 minutes. Roll out the dough between two sheets of baking paper to fit the dish. Line the dish with the dough and trim the edges. Refrigerate for 20 minutes.

Cover the pastry with crumpled baking paper and fill with baking beads or rice. Bake for 15 minutes, then remove the paper and beads and bake for 15–20 minutes, or until the base is dry. Cool completely.

Place the pie dish on a flat baking tray to catch any drips. Spread the pecans and chocolate over the pastry base. Whisk together the sugar, corn syrup, eggs and vanilla in a jug. Pour into the pastry shell and bake for 45 minutes (the filling will still be a bit wobbly, but will set on cooling). Cool before cutting to serve.

PREPARATION TIME: 45 MINUTES   COOKING TIME: 1 HOUR 20 MINUTES

COCOA AND DATE CROSTATA

SWEET SHORTCRUST PASTRY
300 g (10½ oz/2⅓ cups) plain
(all-purpose) flour, sifted
125 g (4½ oz/1 cup) icing (confectioners')
sugar, sifted
150 g (5½ oz) unsalted butter,
chilled and chopped
1 large egg yolk

500 g (1 lb 2 oz/2¾ cups) dried
dates, pitted
½ teaspoon vanilla extract
2 teaspoons grated lemon zest
½ teaspoon ground cinnamon
½ teaspoon ground ginger
30 g (1 oz/¼ cup) unsweetened
cocoa powder
1 tablespoon soft brown sugar
¼ teaspoon bicarbonate of soda
(baking soda)
1 egg yolk, at room temperature
1 teaspoon caster (superfine) sugar
¼ teaspoon ground cinnamon
cream, to serve

SERVES 12

Preheat the oven to 180°C (350°F/Gas 4). Grease a 25 cm (10 inch) loose-based round tart tin.

To make the pastry, put the flour, icing sugar, butter and a pinch of salt in the food processor. Using the pulse button, process until the mixture resembles coarse breadcrumbs. Combine the egg yolk with 1-2 tablespoon chilled water in a small bowl. Add to the flour mixture and, using the pulse button, process until a dough forms, being careful not to overprocess. If the dough is dry and not coming together, add a little more water, 1 teaspoon at a time. Turn out onto a lightly floured work surface and press the dough into a flat, round disc. Cover with plastic wrap and refrigerate for 30 minutes.

Put the dates, vanilla, zest, cinnamon, ginger, cocoa, brown sugar and 250 ml (9 fl oz/1 cup) water in a saucepan over medium heat. Bring to a simmer, then add the bicarbonate of soda, stir and set aside to cool. Transfer the mixture to a food processor. Using the pulse button, mix to form a coarse paste.

Using two-thirds of the pastry, roll out enough to fit the base and side of the tin. Roll out the remaining pastry to form a round that is large enough for the top. Spoon the filling over the pastry base, smoothing the top.

Combine the egg yolk with 1 tablespoon water and brush the edges with the egg wash. Place the pastry round over the date filling, gently pressing to remove any air bubbles, and pressing the edges of the pastry together to seal. Cut a slit in the middle of the pastry to allow steam to escape, then brush the top with the remaining egg wash. Combine the sugar and cinnamon and sprinkle it over the top.

Bake for 1 hour, or until golden. Cool completely before removing from the tin. Serve with cream.

PREPARATION TIME: 20 MINUTES +   COOKING TIME: 1 HOUR 10 MINUTES

SICILIAN CANNOLI

PASTRY
250 g (9 oz/2 cups) plain (all-purpose) flour
2 teaspoons instant coffee granules
2 teaspoons unsweetened cocoa powder
2 tablespoons caster (superfine) sugar
60 g (2¼ oz) unsalted butter, chilled and chopped

FILLING
250 g (9 oz) ricotta cheese
185 g (6½ oz/1½ cups) icing (confectioners') sugar
1 teaspoon orange flower water
30 g (1 oz/¼ cup) grated dark chocolate
60 g (2¼ oz) candied citrus peel
icing (confectioners') sugar, to dust

MAKES 18

To make the pastry, combine the flour, coffee, cocoa, sugar and a pinch of salt. Rub the butter into the flour to make fine breadcrumbs, then work in up to 125 ml (4 fl oz/½ cup) water to make a soft dough. Knead lightly and divide in two. Roll each half out between two sheets of baking paper until about 3 mm (⅛ inch) thick. Cut into 18 (7½ cm/2¾ inch) squares. Place metal cannoli moulds or cannelloni pasta tubes diagonally across the squares and fold the corners across to overlap in the middle. Moisten the overlapping dough, then press firmly to seal. (If you use cannelloni pasta tubes, discard them after frying.)

In a saucepan, deep-fry the tubes, a few at a time, in hot oil deep enough to cover them. When golden and crisp, remove and leave to cool, still on their moulds.

To make the filling, beat the ricotta, icing sugar and orange flower water until smooth. Fold in the chocolate and candied peel. Refrigerate until set.

Slide the pastry tubes off the moulds. Using a piping (icing) bag or a spoon, stuff the tubes with filling, leaving some exposed at each end. Dust with icing sugar before serving.

PREPARATION TIME: 40 MINUTES   COOKING TIME: 10 MINUTES

CHOCOLATE TART

375 g (13 oz) shortcrust pastry
50 g (1¾ oz/⅓ cup) chopped dark chocolate
400 g (14 oz/2⅔ cups) chopped milk chocolate
300 ml (10½ fl oz) thick (double/heavy) cream

SERVES 12

Preheat the oven to 200°C (400°F/Gas 6). Grease a 35 x 11 cm (14 x 4¼ inch) loose-based rectangular tart tin.

Roll out the pastry on a lightly floured work surface until 3 mm (⅛ inch) thick, to fit the base and sides of the tin. Roll the pastry onto the rolling pin, then lift and ease it into the tin, gently pressing to fit into the corners. Trim the edges, cover with plastic wrap and refrigerate for 1 hour.

Line the pastry shell with a piece of baking paper and cover the base with baking beads or uncooked rice. Bake the pastry for 10 minutes, then remove the paper and beads and bake for a further 10 minutes, or until the pastry is golden.

Put the dark chocolate in a heatproof bowl. Half fill a saucepan with water, bring to the boil, then remove from the heat and sit the bowl over the pan (don't let the bowl touch the water or the chocolate will get too hot and seize). Stir occasionally until the chocolate melts. Brush the base of the pastry with the melted chocolate.

Put the milk chocolate and cream in a small heatproof bowl. Sit the bowl over a small saucepan of simmering water, stirring until the chocolate has melted and the mixture is smooth. Allow the chocolate to cool slightly, then pour into the pastry case. Refrigerate overnight, or until the chocolate filling has set. Serve the tart in small slices as it is very rich.

PREPARATION TIME: 30 MINUTES   COOKING TIME: 30 MINUTES

PROFITEROLES WITH COFFEE MASCARPONE AND DARK CHOCOLATE SAUCE

125 g (4½ oz/1 cup) plain (all-purpose) flour
70 g (2½ oz) unsalted butter, cubed
4 eggs, at room temperature

FILLING
2 tablespoons instant coffee granules
450 g (1 lb/2 cups) mascarpone cheese
2 tablespoons icing (confectioners') sugar

DARK CHOCOLATE SAUCE
100 g (3½ oz/²/₃ cup) chopped dark chocolate
30 g (1 oz) unsalted butter
80 ml (2½ fl oz/¹/₃ cup) cream

MAKES 16

Preheat the oven to 200°C (400°F/Gas 6). Lightly grease two baking trays. Sift the flour onto a piece of baking paper.

Put the butter, ½ teaspoon salt and 250 ml (9 fl oz/1 cup) water in a saucepan and bring to the boil, stirring occasionally. Using the baking paper as a funnel, quickly pour the flour into the boiling mixture. Reduce the heat to low, then beat vigorously until the mixture leaves the side of the pan and forms a smooth ball.

Transfer the mixture to a bowl and set aside to cool a little. Using electric beaters, beat in the eggs, one at a time, until the mixture is thick and glossy.

Using two spoons, gently drop 16 rounded balls of the mixture about 3 cm (1¼ inches) in diameter and 3 cm (1¼ inches) apart onto the prepared baking trays. Bake for 20 minutes, or until the balls are puffed. Reduce the oven to 180°C (350°F/Gas 4) and bake for 10 minutes, or until the puffs are golden brown and crisp.

Using a small, sharp knife, gently slit the puffs to allow the steam to escape, then return them to the oven for 10 minutes, or until the insides are dry. Cool to room temperature.

To make the filling, dissolve the coffee in 1 tablespoon boiling water. Set aside to cool. Combine the coffee, mascarpone and icing sugar. Be careful not to overmix, or the mixture will separate.

To make the dark chocolate sauce, put the chocolate, butter and cream in a small heatproof bowl set over a small saucepan of simmering water. Mix well then set aside to cool slightly.

Just before serving, cut the profiteroles in half and sandwich together with the filling. Drizzle with the chocolate sauce.

PREPARATION TIME: 40 MINUTES   COOKING TIME: 45 MINUTES

CHOCOLATE RICOTTA TART

185 g (6½ oz/1½ cups) plain
(all-purpose) flour
100 g (3½ oz) unsalted butter, chopped
2 tablespoons caster (superfine) sugar

FILLING
1.25 kg (2 lb 12 oz) ricotta cheese
125 g (4 oz/½ cup) caster
(superfine) sugar
2 tablespoons plain (all-purpose) flour
1 teaspoon instant coffee granules
125 g (4½ oz) finely chopped chocolate
4 egg yolks, at room temperature
40 g (1¼ oz) chocolate, extra
½ teaspoon vegetable oil

SERVES 8–10

To make the pastry, sift the flour into a large bowl and add the butter. Rub the butter into the flour with your fingertips, until fine and crumbly. Stir in the sugar. Add 60 ml (2 fl oz/¼ cup) cold water and cut with a knife to form a dough, adding a little more water if necessary. Turn out onto a lightly floured surface and gather into a ball.

Lightly grease a 25 cm (10 inch) spring-form cake tin. Roll out the dough, then line the tin so that the pastry comes about two-thirds of the way up the side. Cover with plastic wrap and refrigerate while making the filling.

Preheat the oven to 180°C (350°F/Gas 4).

To make the filling, combine the ricotta, sugar, flour and a pinch of salt until smooth. Dissolve the coffee in 2 teaspoons hot water. Stir into the ricotta mixture, with the chocolate and egg yolks, until well mixed. Spoon into the chilled pastry shell and smooth the surface. Chill for 30 minutes, or until firm.

Put the cake tin on a baking tray. Bake for 1 hour, or until firm. Turn off the oven and leave the tart in the oven to cool with the door ajar (the tart may crack slightly but this will not be noticeable when it cools and has been decorated).

To decorate, melt the extra chocolate and stir in the oil. With a fork, flick thin drizzles of melted chocolate over the tart, or pipe over for a neater finish. Cool completely before cutting into wedges for serving.

PREPARATION TIME: 20 MINUTES +   COOKING TIME: 1 HOUR

67

CHOCOLATE ORANGE TARTS

90 g (3¼ oz/¾ cup) plain (all-purpose)
flour, sifted
50 g (1¾ oz/¼ cup) rice flour,
55 g (2 oz/½ cup) ground almonds
1 tablespoon sugar
125 g (4½ oz) unsalted butter, chopped
1 egg yolk, at room temperature

FILLING
100 g (3½ oz/⅔ cup) chopped
dark chocolate
110 g (3¾ oz/¾ cup) chopped
milk chocolate
1 teaspoon grated orange zest
2 tablespoons orange juice

310 ml (10¾ fl oz/1¼ cups) cream
2 eggs, at room temperature
3 egg yolks, at room temperature, whisked

whipped cream and candied orange zest,
to serve
icing (confectioners') sugar, to dust

SERVES 6

Preheat the oven to 180°C (350°F/Gas 4). Brush six 12 cm (4 inch) individual fluted flan tins with melted butter.

In a food processor, process the flours, a pinch of salt, the ground almonds, sugar and butter for 20 seconds, or until fine and crumbly. Add the egg yolk and 1–2 tablespoons cold water. Process until the dough comes together. Divide the dough into six even portions then roll out between two sheets of baking paper to a 6 mm (¼ inch) thickness. Line the tart tins with the dough, and trim the edges with a sharp knife. Refrigerate for 20 minutes.

Cut six sheets of baking paper large enough to cover the pastry-lined tins. Lay the paper over the pastry and spread with an even layer of baking beads or rice. Bake for for 15 minutes, then discard the beads and paper and bake for another 5 minutes.

To make the filling, put the chocolate in a heatproof bowl. Half fill a saucepan with water, bring to the boil, then remove from the heat and sit the bowl over the pan (don't let the bowl touch the water or the chocolate will get too hot and seize). Stir occasionally until the chocolate melts, then remove from the heat.

Whisk together the orange zest, juice, cream, eggs and egg yolks. Gradually add to the melted chocolate, whisking constantly. Pour the mixture into the pastry cases and bake for 20–25 minutes, or until just set (the filling will set more as the tarts cool). Serve warm with whipped cream and candied orange zest and dust with icing sugar.

PREPARATION TIME: 45 MINUTES   COOKING TIME: 50 MINUTES

CHEESECAKES WITH MIXED BERRIES

4 butternut biscuits
85 g (2 oz/½ cup) white
chocolate chips
250 g (9 oz/1 cup) cream cheese,
at room temperature
60 ml (2 fl oz/¼ cup) cream, for whipping
115 g (4 oz/½ cup) caster
(superfine) sugar
1 egg, at room temperature
250 g (9 oz/1½–2 cups) mixed berries,
such as raspberries, blueberries
and sliced strawberries
Framboise or Cointreau

SERVES 4

Preheat the oven to 160°C (315°F/Gas 2–3). Grease a four-hole muffin tray and line each with two strips of baking paper to make a cross pattern.

Put a biscuit in the base of each hole. Put the chocolate in a heatproof bowl. Half fill a saucepan with water, bring to the boil, then remove from the heat and sit the bowl over the pan (don't let the bowl touch the water or the chocolate will get too hot and seize). Stir occasionally until the chocolate melts.

Using electric beaters, beat the cream cheese, cream and half the sugar until thick and smooth. Beat in the egg and then the melted chocolate. Pour evenly into the muffin holes and bake for 25 minutes, or until set. Cool completely in the tray, then carefully run a small spatula or flat-bladed knife around the edge and lift out of the holes using the paper strips as handles. Refrigerate for 1 hour, or until ready to serve.

Place the berries in a bowl and fold in the remaining sugar. Leave for 10–15 minutes, or until juices form. Flavour with a little liqueur. Serve the cheesecakes topped with the berries.

PREPARATION TIME: 20 MINUTES +   COOKING TIME: 30 MINUTES

CHOCOLATE RAISIN SCROLLS

375 g (1 lb/3 cups) plain (all-purpose) flour, sifted
2 tablespoons caster (superfine) sugar
2 teaspoons dried yeast
finely grated zest of 1 lemon
185 ml (6 fl oz/$^3/_4$ cup) lukewarm milk
125 g (4$^1/_2$ oz) unsalted butter, diced and softened
2 egg yolks, at room temperature, lightly whisked
icing (confectioners') sugar, to dust

FILLING
100 g (3$^1/_2$ oz/$^2/_3$ cup) chopped dark chocolate
90 g (3$^1/_4$ oz/$^3/_4$ cup) raisins
80 g (2$^3/_4$ oz/$^3/_4$ cup) chopped toasted pecans
55 g (2 oz/$^1/_4$ cup) soft brown sugar
60 g (2$^1/_4$ oz) unsalted butter, finely diced

SERVES 8

Mix together the flour, sugar, yeast, $^1/_2$ teaspoon salt and lemon zest and make a well in the centre. Add the milk, butter and egg yolks. Use a wooden spoon and then your hands to mix a soft, but not sticky, dough.

Turn the dough onto a lightly floured surface and knead for 5 minutes or until smooth and elastic. Grease a bowl with unsalted butter. Shape the dough into a ball, place in the bowl and cover with plastic wrap. Place in a warm, draught-free place for 1$^1/_2$ hours or until doubled in size.

To make the filling, combine the chocolate, raisins, pecans, brown sugar and unsalted butter. Stir until evenly combined. Set aside.

Place eight 185 ml (6$^1/_2$ fl oz/$^3/_4$ cup) straight-sided paper cups on a baking tray.

Use your fist to knock down the dough. Knead on a lightly floured surface for 2 minutes, or until returned to its original size. Use a lightly floured rolling pin to roll the dough to a 25 cm x 45 cm (10 x 8 inch) rectangle with a long side closest to you. Spread the filling evenly over the dough, leaving a 5 cm (2 inch) border along the top end. Starting with the long side closest to you, roll up the dough to enclose the filling. Cut the roll into eight even slices, each about 5 cm (2 inch) thick, and place, cut side up, into the paper cases. Brush the tops with milk and cover with plastic wrap. Place in a warm, draught-free place for 30 minutes or until well risen.

Preheat oven to 190°C (375°F/Gas 5). Brush the scrolls again with a little milk and bake for 10 minutes. Reduce the oven to 180°C (350°F/Gas 4) and cook for a further 15 minutes, or until the scrolls are golden and cooked through. Serve warm.

PREPARATION TIME: 20 MINUTES +   COOKING TIME: 1 HOUR 25 MINUTES

THREE CHOCOLATES TART

PASTRY

150 g (5½ oz/1¼ cups) plain
(all-purpose) flour
20 g (¾ oz) unsweetened cocoa powder
75 g (2½ oz) unsalted butter,
chilled and cubed
3 tablespoons caster (superfine) sugar
4 egg yolks, at room temperature
¼ teaspoon vanilla extract

FILLING

110 g (3¾ oz/¾ cup) chopped
white chocolate
3 tablespoons liquid glucose
200 g (7 oz/1⅓ cups) chopped
dark chocolate
300 ml (10½ fl oz) cream, for whipping

GANACHE

30 g (1 oz/¼ cup) chopped
dark chocolate
15 g (½ oz) unsalted butter
1 tablespoon cream

SERVES 8

To make the pastry, process the flour, cocoa and unsalted butter in a food processor to form fine breadcrumbs. Add the sugar using the pulse action, then add the egg yolks, vanilla and 1 tablespoon water. Process to form a smooth dough. Flatten to a disc, cover with plastic wrap and chill for 45 minutes.

Preheat the oven to 180°C (350°F/Gas 4). Grease a 20 cm (8 inch) loose-based tart tin. Roll the pastry out thinly between two sheets of baking paper and use to line the prepared tin, pressing it into the flutes. Cover with a sheet of baking paper, fill with baking beads or rice and bake for 12 minutes. Remove the baking paper and beads and bake for about 5 minutes more, or until crisp and dry. Cool completely.

To make the filling, put the white chocolate in a bowl set over a saucepan of simmering water. Don't let the bowl touch the water or the chocolate will get too hot and seize. Heat until melted and smooth. Spoon into the tart case and spread evenly over the base using the back of a spoon. Cool until set.

Put the glucose and dark chocolate in a heatproof bowl set over a saucepan of simmering water. Heat, stirring often, until melted. It will be very thick and tacky. Allow to cool. Whip the cream until stiff peaks form. Fold a heaped spoonful of cream into the chocolate mixture to loosen it. Add the rest of the cream and fold through; the mixture will become very smooth and glossy. Spoon into the tart case, leaving it in broad swirls across the surface. Refrigerate until set.

To make the ganache, put the chocolate, butter and cream in a small bowl set over a saucepan of simmering water. Stir until smooth and glossy. Remove from the heat and cool. Spoon the ganache into a piping (icing) bag fitted with a 1–2 mm (1/16 inch) tip. Pipe a criss-cross pattern, like an uneven grid, over the tart. Refrigerate before serving to set.

PREPARATION TIME: 30 MINUTES +   COOKING TIME: 35 MINUTES

BAKED CHOCOLATE CHEESECAKE

125 g (4½ oz) plain chocolate biscuits
40 g (1½ oz/¼ cup) chopped almonds
90 g (3¼ oz) unsalted butter, melted
1 tablespoon soft brown sugar

FILLING
500 g (1 lb 2 oz/2 cups) cream cheese,
at room temperature
95 g (3¼ oz/½ cup) soft brown sugar
110 g (3¾ oz/¾ cup) chopped dark
chocolate
125 ml (4 fl oz/½ cup) thick
(double/heavy) cream
2 eggs, at room temperature, beaten
1 teaspoon grated orange zest
whipped cream, to serve
raspberries, to serve
chocolate curls, to serve

SERVES 8–10

Brush a 20 cm (8 inch) spring-form cake tin with melted butter or oil and line the base with baking paper. Put the biscuits in a food processor with the almonds and process into crumbs.

Add the butter and sugar and process until they are combined. Press the mixture firmly into the base of the tin and refrigerate until firm. Preheat the oven to 160°C (315°F/Gas 2–3).

Put the chocolate in a heatproof bowl. Half fill a saucepan with water, bring to the boil, then remove from the heat and sit the bowl over the pan (don't let the bowl touch the water or the chocolate will get too hot and seize). Stir occasionally until the chocolate melts. Allow to cool.

To make the filling, beat the cream cheese and sugar together until creamy. Blend in the cooled melted chocolate, cream, eggs and orange zest and then mix until smooth.

Pour the filling over the crumb crust and smooth the surface. Bake for 1 hour 20 minutes, or until the filling is firm to the touch.

Leave the cheesecake to cool in the tin and then refrigerate overnight. Top with whipped cream, fresh raspberries and chocolate curls. Cut into thick wedges and serve.

PREPARATION TIME: 20 MINUTES +   COOKING TIME: 1 HOUR 40 MINUTES

CHOCOLATE AND PEANUT BUTTER PIE

200 g (7 oz/1½ cups) crushed chocolate biscuits with cream centre

50 g (1¾ oz) unsalted butter, melted

185 g (7 oz/¾ cup) cream cheese, at room temperature

85 g (3 oz/⅔ cup) icing (confectioners') sugar, sifted

100 g (3½ oz/⅔ cup) smooth peanut butter

1 teaspoon vanilla extract

250 ml (9 fl oz/1 cup) cream, whipped to firm peaks

60 ml (2 fl oz/¼ cup) cream, extra

15 g (½ oz) unsalted butter, extra

50 g (1¾ oz) grated dark chocolate

honey-roasted peanuts, chopped, to garnish

SERVES 10–12

Combine the biscuit crumbs with the butter and press into the base of a 23 x 18 x 3 cm (9 x 7 x 1¼ in) pie dish and refrigerate for 15 minutes, or until firm.

Beat the cream cheese and icing sugar with electric beaters until smooth. Add the peanut butter and vanilla and beat together. Stir in a third of the whipped cream until smooth, then gently fold in the remaining whipped cream. Pour into the pie shell. Refrigerate for 2 hours, or until firm.

Place the extra cream and butter in a saucepan and stir over medium heat until the butter is melted and the mixture just comes to a simmer. Remove from the heat, add the grated chocolate and stir until melted. Cool a little, then drizzle the chocolate over the top of the pie to create a lattice pattern. Refrigerate for 2 hours, or until the cream cheese filling and chocolate are firm.

Remove the pie from the fridge, scatter over the chopped peanuts and serve.

PREPARATION TIME: 20 MINUTES +   COOKING TIME: 5 MINUTES

BANANA CREAM PIE

375 g (13 oz) shortcrust pastry
80 g (2¾ oz/½ cup) dark chocolate chips
4 egg yolks, at room temperature
115 g (4 oz/½ cup) caster
(superfine) sugar
½ teaspoon vanilla extract
2 tablespoons custard powder
500 ml (17 fl oz/2 cups) milk
40 g (1½ oz) unsalted butter, softened
1 teaspoon brandy or rum
3 large ripe bananas, cut into 3–4 mm
(¼ inch) slices
sliced banana, extra, to decorate
1 tablespoon grated dark chocolate,
to decorate

SERVES 6–8

Roll out the pastry between two sheets of baking paper to line the base of a 23 x 18 x 3 cm (9 x 7 x 1¼ inch) baking dish. Remove the top sheet of paper and invert the pastry into the tin. Trim the excess and refrigerate for 20 minutes.

Preheat the oven to 190°C (375°F/Gas 5). Line the pastry with crumpled baking paper and cover with baking beads or rice. Bake for 10 minutes, remove the paper and beads, then bake for a further 10 minutes, or until the pastry is dry and cooked through. While still hot, cover with the chocolate chips. Leave for 5 minutes to soften, then spread the melted chocolate over the base.

Beat the egg yolks, sugar, vanilla and custard powder with electric beaters for 2–3 minutes, or until thick. Bring the milk to the boil in a saucepan over medium heat, remove from the heat and gradually pour into the egg mixture, stirring well. Return the custard filling to the saucepan and bring to the boil, stirring well for 2 minutes, or until thick. Remove from the heat, stir in the butter and brandy, stirring until the butter has melted, then leave to cool. Arrange the banana slices over the chocolate, then pour over the custard. Decorate with the extra banana and grated chocolate.

PREPARATION TIME: 20 MINUTES +   COOKING TIME: 25 MINUTES

CHOCOLATE MOUSSE FLAN

200 g (7 oz/1½ cups) chocolate
biscuit crumbs
100 g (3½ oz) unsalted butter, melted

CHOCOLATE CREAM
100 g (3½ oz/⅔ cup) chopped dark
chocolate
50 ml (1¾ fl oz/¼ cup) cream

MOCHA MOUSSE
200 g (7 oz) dark chocolate, melted
60 g (2¼ oz) unsalted butter, melted
50 ml (1¾ fl oz/¼) cup thick
(double/heavy) cream
2 egg yolks, at room temperature
2 teaspoons instant coffee powder
2 teaspoons powdered gelatine
unsweetened cocoa powder, to dust

SERVES 8–10

Brush a 23 cm (9 inch) round, loose-based, fluted flan tin with melted butter or oil.

Combine the biscuit crumbs and butter. Press into the base and side of the tin. Refrigerate for 20 minutes, or until firm.

To make the chocolate cream, place the chocolate and cream in a heatproof bowl and set the bowl over a pan of simmering water until the chocolate melts and is smooth. Spread evenly over the flan base. Refrigerate until set.

To make the mocha mousse, combine the chocolate, butter, cream and egg yolks. Meanwhile, combine the coffee and 1 teaspoon boiling water then add to mixture.

Sprinkle the gelatine over 1 tablespoon water in a small bowl. Stand the bowl in a pan of hot water and stir until the gelatine dissolves. Add the gelatine to the chocolate and stir until smooth.

Using electric beaters, beat the cream until soft peaks form, then fold into the chocolate. Spread over the flan and refrigerate until set.

Cut a star-shaped stencil from stiff cardboard. Place the stencil over the flan and dust with cocoa powder. Carefully lift off the stencil. Slice the flan into wedges.

PREPARATION TIME: 35 MINUTES +   COOKING TIME: 5 MINUTES

CHOCOLATE BREAD

2½ teaspoons instant dried yeast
55 g (2 oz/¼ cup) caster (superfine) sugar
90 g (3¼ oz) roughly chopped dark chocolate
50 g (1¾ oz) unsalted butter
375 g (13 oz/3 cups) white bread (strong) flour
30 g (1 oz/¼ cup) unsweetened cocoa powder
1 egg, at room temperature, lightly beaten
½ teaspoon vanilla extract
90 g (3¼ oz/½ cup) dark chocolate chips

SERVES 8–10

Sprinkle the yeast and a pinch of the sugar over 185 ml (6 fl oz/¾ cup) warm water in a small bowl. Stir to dissolve the sugar, then leave in a draught-free place for 10 minutes, or until the yeast is foamy.

Put the chocolate and butter in a heatproof bowl. Sit the bowl over a saucepan of simmering water, stirring frequently until the chocolate and butter have melted. Don't let the bowl touch the water or the chocolate will get too hot and seize.

Combine the flour, cocoa, ¼ teaspoon salt and the remaining sugar with an electric mixer with a dough hook attachment. Combine the egg and vanilla with the chocolate and butter, then pour the chocolate mixture and yeast into the flour. With the mixer set to the lowest speed, mix for 1–2 minutes, or until a dough forms. Increase the speed to medium and knead the dough for another 10 minutes, or until the dough is smooth and elastic. Alternatively, mix the dough by hand using a wooden spoon, then turn it out onto a floured work surface and knead for 10 minutes, or until the dough is smooth and elastic.

Grease a large bowl with oil, then transfer the dough to the bowl, turning the dough to coat it in the oil. Cover with plastic wrap and leave to rise in a draught-free place for 1½–2 hours, or until the dough has doubled in size.

Knock back the dough by punching it gently, then turn it out onto a floured work surface. Divide the dough in half. Gently press out each half until 1 cm (½ inch) thick, then scatter the chocolate chips over each half of the dough. Roll up each piece to form a log. Transfer to a greased baking tray. Cover with a damp cloth and leave for 1 hour, or until doubled in size. Meanwhile, preheat the oven to 180°C (350°F/Gas 4). Bake for 45–50 minutes, or until the bread is light brown and sounds hollow when tapped on the base. Transfer to a wire rack to cool. This chocolate bread is not overly sweet, so serve freshly sliced or toasted with sweetened mascarpone.

PREPARATION TIME: 30 MINUTES +   COOKING TIME: 55 MINUTES

CHOCOLATE HONEYCOMB PASTRIES

2 x 24 cm (9½ inch) square sheets
ready-rolled frozen puff pastry
75 g (2 oz/½ cup) finely chopped
dark chocolate
50 g (1¾ oz) chopped honeycomb
milk, to brush
icing (confectioners') sugar, to dust

MAKES 18

Preheat the oven to 220°C (425°F/Gas 7). Line two baking trays with baking paper.

Lay the puff pastry on a cutting board and cut each sheet into nine 8 cm (3¼ inch) squares. Set aside for 3–5 minutes, or until thawed slightly.

Meanwhile, combine the chocolate and honeycomb. Divide between the pastry squares, placing the chocolate and honeycomb down the centre on one half.

Fold the pastry squares in half to enclose the filling and then press the edges firmly with a fork to seal. Place the pastries on the baking trays about 3 cm (1¼ inch) apart and brush with a little milk.

Bake for 15–18 minutes, or until golden and puffed. Cool slightly before serving, sprinkled with icing sugar.

PREPARATION TIME: 20 MINUTES   COOKING TIME: 18 MINUTES

CARAMEL TARTS WITH CHOCOLATE GANACHE

GANACHE
100 g (3½ oz/⅔ cup) chopped dark chocolate
2 tablespoons cream

PASTRY
150 g (5½ oz/1¼ cups) plain (all-purpose) flour
90 g (3¼ oz) unsalted butter, chilled and cubed
65 g (¼ oz/heaped ¼ cup) caster (superfine) sugar

FILLING
395 g (13¾ oz) tin sweetened condensed milk
30 g (1 oz) unsalted butter
2 tablespoons golden syrup (light treacle)
1½ tablespoons chopped pistachio nuts, to garnish

MAKES 12

To make the ganache, melt the chocolate and cream in a bowl over a saucepan of simmering water, stirring well until melted. Don't let the bowl touch the water or the chocolate will get too hot and seize. Remove from the heat, cool, then refrigerate for 10–15 minutes until firm but not solid.

Preheat the oven to 180°C (350°F/Gas 4). Grease a 12-hole mini muffin tray. Run a strip of foil across the base and up two sides of each hole, leaving a bit of foil to hang over the sides. These will act as handles to help the removal of the tarts later on.

To make the pastry, put the flour, butter and sugar into a food processor and pulse until the mixture resembles breadcrumbs. Divide among the muffin holes and firmly press the mixture down into the bases with your fingers. Bake for 12–15 minutes, or until lightly golden in colour. While they are still hot, press the bases down with the back of a small teaspoon, as they will have risen a little.

To make the filling, put the condensed milk, butter and golden syrup in a saucepan over low heat. Stir until the butter has melted. Increase the heat to medium and simmer for 2–3 minutes, stirring constantly, until light caramel in colour. When stirring, ensure that the bottom and side of the pan are scraped to prevent the mixture from catching and scorching.

Divide the caramel among the pastry bases and cool for 5 minutes. Gently remove the tarts from the tin, then transfer to a wire rack to cool completely.

To serve, whisk the ganache well. Put into a piping (icing) bag with a medium-sized star nozzle and pipe swirls on top of the caramel. Sprinkle with the pistachios. Store in the refrigerator, covered, until set. Remove from the refrigerator 10–15 minutes before serving.

PREPARATION TIME: 25 MINUTES +   COOKING TIME: 25 MINUTES

COLD AND CREAMY

RUM CHOCOLATE MOUSSE

250 g (9 oz/1²/₃ cups) chopped dark chocolate

3 eggs, at room temperature

60 g (2¹/₄ oz/¹/₄ cup) caster (superfine) sugar

2 teaspoons dark rum

250 ml (9 fl oz/1 cup) cream, for whipping

whipped cream, to serve

grated dark chocolate, to serve

SERVES 4

Put the chocolate in a heatproof bowl. Half fill a saucepan with water and bring to the boil. Remove from the heat and place the bowl over the pan. Don't let the bowl touch the water or the chocolate will get too hot and seize. Stir occasionally until the chocolate has melted. Leave to cool.

Using electric beaters, beat the eggs and sugar in a bowl for 5 minutes, or until thick, pale and increased in volume.

Using a metal spoon, fold in the melted chocolate with the rum, leave to cool, then gently fold in the lightly whipped cream.

Spoon into four 250 ml (9 fl oz/1 cup) ramekins or dessert glasses. Refrigerate for 2 hours, or until set. Serve with extra whipped cream and grated chocolate.

PREPARATION TIME: 20 MINUTES   COOKING TIME: 5 MINUTES

KAHLÚA CHOCOLATE PARFAIT

125 g (4¹/₂ oz) chocolate and vanilla cream biscuits, chopped

2 tablespoons Kahlúa or other coffee liqueur

500 ml (17 fl oz/2 cups) chocolate ice cream

250 ml (9 fl oz/1 cup) cream, whipped

50 g (1³/₄ oz/¹/₃ cup) chocolate chips

SERVES 4

Mix together the biscuits and liqueur. Set aside for 5 minutes for the biscuits to absorb the liqueur.

In each of four tall parfait glasses, layer the ice cream, biscuit mixture, cream and chocolate chips. Continue until the glasses are full.

Top with whipped cream and a few chocolate chips. Serve immediately.

PREPARATION TIME: 10 MINUTES   COOKING TIME: NIL

CHUNKY MONKEY PARFAIT

CHOCOLATE FUDGE SAUCE
100 g (3½ oz/⅔ cup) chopped
dark chocolate
185 ml (6 fl oz/¾ cup) sweetened
condensed milk
80 ml (2½ fl oz/⅓ cup) cream
40 g (1½ oz) unsalted butter, diced

MARSHMALLOW FLUFF
90 g (3¼ oz/1 cup) white marshmallows
80 ml (2½ fl oz/⅓ cup) cream

6 scoops chocolate-chip ice cream
6 large pretzels
6 scoops praline ice cream
10 chocolate-coated peanut butter
cups, chopped
6 scoops peanut butter ice cream
50 g (1¾ oz/⅓ cup) honey-roasted
peanuts

SERVES 6

To make the chocolate fudge sauce, put the chocolate, condensed milk and cream into a heatproof bowl. Fill a saucepan one-third full with water and bring to a simmer over medium heat. Sit the bowl on top of the saucepan. Stir occasionally until the chocolate has almost melted, then remove from the heat and stir until completely smooth. Beat in the butter until melted and the mixture smooth. Set aside to cool for about 20 minutes, stirring regularly.

To make the marshmallow fluff, finely chop the marshmallows, put them in a saucepan with the cream and melt over low heat until the marshmallows are completely dissolved. Allow to cool, then put in the fridge to chill.

To assemble the sundaes, put a tablespoon of chocolate fudge sauce in each of six tall parfait glasses. Top each with a scoop of chocolate-chip ice cream, some pretzels, a scoop of praline ice cream, some chopped peanut butter cups, then a scoop of the peanut butter ice cream. Press down lightly.

Dollop with the marshmallow fluff. Serve drizzled with extra chocolate fudge sauce and scattered with honey-roasted peanuts.

PREPARATION TIME: 20 MINUTES   COOKING TIME: 10 MINUTES

WHITE CHOCOLATE AND COCONUT SEMIFREDDO WITH BLACKBERRIES

170 ml (5½ fl oz/⅔ cup) milk
45 g (1¾ oz/½ cup) desiccated coconut
100 g (3½ oz/⅔ cup) chopped white chocolate
2 egg yolks, at room temperature
55 g (2 oz/¼ cup) caster (superfine) sugar
185 ml (6 fl oz/¾ cup) cream, lightly whipped

BLACKBERRIES IN SYRUP
2 tablespoons caster (superfine) sugar
300 g (10½ oz) blackberries

SERVES 8

Spray a 750 ml (26 fl oz/3 cup) bar (loaf) tin with oil, then line it with plastic wrap (the oil will help you get the creases out of the wrap, so your semifreddo will have a smoother finish). Leave the wrap to hang over the sides of the tin.

Put the milk and coconut in a saucepan over medium heat and bring to a simmer. Remove from the heat, cover and cool to room temperature. Strain through a fine sieve, pressing with the back of a spoon to extract as much milk as possible. There should be about 80 ml (2½ fl oz/⅓ cup).

Put the chocolate in a saucepan over low heat, stir in the infused milk stirring until the chocolate melts. Remove from the heat.

Whisk the egg yolks and sugar in a heatproof bowl over a pan of simmering water until very thick and pale. Stir in the chocolate mixture. Fold in the whipped cream in two batches. Pour into the tin and smooth the surface. Cover with the overhanging plastic wrap and freeze for 6 hours, or until frozen.

Just before serving prepare the blackberries. Put the sugar in a small pan with 2 tablespoons of water and stir over low heat until the sugar has dissolved. Bring to a simmer, add the blackberries and briefly warm through.

Tip out the semifreddo onto a chopping board and peel away the plastic wrap. Cut into slices and serve immediately with the blackberries and syrup.

PREPARATION TIME: 30 MINUTES   COOKING TIME: 20 MINUTES

BAKED CHOCOLATE CUSTARDS

30 g (1 oz) unsalted butter, melted
55 g (2 oz/¼ cup) caster (superfine) sugar, for dusting
300 ml (10½ fl oz) cream
200 ml (7 fl oz) milk
200 g (7 oz/1⅓ cups) roughly chopped dark chocolate
grated zest of 1 orange
6 eggs, at room temperature
115 g (4 oz/½ cup) caster (superfine) sugar, extra
raspberries, to serve
icing (confectioners') sugar, for dusting

SERVES 10

Preheat the oven to 160°C (315°F/Gas 2–3). Grease ten 125 ml (4 fl oz/ ½ cup) ramekins with butter and dust the inside of each one with caster sugar.

Put the cream and milk in a saucepan over low heat and bring almost to the boil. Add the chocolate and stir over low heat until the chocolate has melted and is well combined. Stir in the orange zest.

Whisk the eggs and extra sugar for 5 minutes, or until pale and thick. Whisk a little of the hot chocolate cream into the eggs, then pour onto the remaining chocolate cream, whisking continuously.

Divide the mixture among the ramekins. Place the ramekins in a roasting tin. Pour enough boiling water into the tin to come halfway up the sides of the ramekins. Cover with foil and bake for 30–35 minutes, or until the custards are set.

Remove the ramekins from the water bath and set aside to cool completely. Turn the custards out onto serving plates. Top with raspberries and dust with icing sugar before serving.

PREPARATION TIME: 20 MINUTES   COOKING TIME: 40 MINUTES

RASPBERRY MERINGUE WHITE CHOCOLATE ROLL

4 egg whites, at room temperature
170 g (6 oz/^{3}/$_4$ cup) caster
(superfine) sugar
125 g (4^1/$_2$ oz) cream cheese, softened
125 g (4^1/$_2$ oz/^{3}/$_4$ cup) white chocolate
185 g (6 oz/^{3}/$_4$ cup) sour cream
125 g (4^1/$_2$ oz/1 cup) raspberries

SERVES 6–8

Preheat the oven to 180°C (350°F/Gas 4). Line the base and long sides of a 25 x 30 cm (10 x 12 inch) roasting tin with baking paper.

Beat the egg whites until soft peaks form. Gradually add the sugar, beating constantly. Beat until the meringue is thick and glossy and the sugar has dissolved.

Spread the mixture into the tin and bake for 10 minutes, or until lightly browned and firm to touch. Quickly and carefully turn onto baking paper that has been sprinkled with caster sugar. Leave to cool.

Put the white chocolate in a heatproof bowl. Half fill a saucepan with water, bring to the boil, then remove from the heat and sit the bowl over the pan (don't let the bowl touch the water or the chocolate will get too hot and seize). Stir occasionally until the chocolate melts. Allow to cool.

Beat the cream cheese and sour cream until smooth and creamy. Add the cooled white chocolate and beat until smooth. Spread over the meringue base, leaving a 1 cm (½ inch) border. Top with a layer of raspberries.

Carefully roll the meringue, using the paper as a guide, from one short end. Wrap firmly in the sugared paper and plastic wrap and chill until firm. Cut into slices to serve.

PREPARATION TIME: 35 MINUTES COOKING TIME: 15 MINUTES

MOCHA COFFEE CREAM POTS

600 ml (21 fl oz) cream
50 g (1³/4 oz/²/3 cup) roasted coffee beans
100 g (3¹/2 oz/²/3 cup) chopped
dark chocolate
6 egg yolks, at room temperature
55 g (2 oz/¹/4 cup) caster (superfine) sugar
3 teaspoons Tia Maria or other
coffee liqueur
whipped cream, to serve
chocolate-coated coffee beans, to serve

SERVES 6

Preheat the oven to 150°C (300°F/Gas 2). Put the cream, coffee beans and chocolate into a saucepan. Stir over low heat until the chocolate melts, then bring to a simmer and cook for 2–3 minutes. Remove from the heat. Leave for 30 minutes to allow the coffee to infuse.

Whisk the egg yolks, sugar and liqueur together, then strain in the coffee-infused milk. Stir, then divide the mixture among six 125 ml (4 fl oz/¹/2 cup) ramekins. Put in a roasting tin and pour enough boiling water into the tin to come halfway up the sides of the ramekins. Bake for 25–30 minutes.

Remove from the oven and leave to cool. Refrigerate overnight until set. Serve with whipped cream and coffee beans.

PREPARATION TIME: 40 MINUTES   COOKING TIME: 35 MINUTES

MARSALA AND HONEY CHOCOLATE SORBET

55 g (2 oz /¹/4 cup) caster (superfine)
sugar
30 g (1 oz/¹/4 cup) unsweetened cocoa
powder, sifted
175 g (6 oz/¹/2 cup) honey
2 tablespoons Marsala
cream, to serve

SERVES 8

Combine the sugar and cocoa in a saucepan and gradually whisk in 625 ml (21¹/2 fl oz/2¹/2 cups) water. Add the honey and stir over medium heat until the sugar and honey dissolves. Bring just to the boil. Remove from the heat, stir in the Marsala and set aside to cool to room temperature. Pour into a 1 litre (35 fl oz/4 cup) freezerproof container. Cover and freeze for 6–8 hours, or until frozen.

Use a metal spoon to break up the frozen mixture. Transfer to a food processor and process to a soft, icy texture (don't overprocess or it will begin to melt). Immediately transfer the sorbet back to the container. Cover and refreeze for 4–6 hours, or until completely frozen. Serve in small scoops and drizzle with cream.

PREPARATION TIME: 20 MINUTES +   COOKING TIME: 10 MINUTES

Mocha coffee cream pots

CHOCOLATE CHERRY TRIFLE

350 g (12 oz) chocolate cake
2 x 450 g (1 lb) tins pitted dark cherries
60 ml (2 fl oz/¼ cup) Kirsch
2 egg yolks, at room temperature
2 tablespoons sugar
1 tablespoon cornflour (cornstarch)
250 ml (9 fl oz/1 cup) milk
1 teaspoon vanilla extract
185 ml (6 fl oz/¾ cup) cream, whipped
whipped cream, to serve
30 g (1 oz) toasted slivered almonds, to serve

SERVES 6

Cut the cake into thin strips. Line the base of a 1.75 (6 fl oz/7 cup) litre serving bowl with a third of the cake.

Drain the cherries, reserving the juice. Combine 250 ml (9 fl oz/1 cup) of the juice with the Kirsch and sprinkle some liberally over the cake. Spoon some cherries over the cake.

To make the custard, whisk the egg yolks, sugar and cornflour in a heatproof bowl until thick and pale. Heat the milk in a saucepan and bring almost to the boil. Remove from the heat and add the milk gradually to the egg mixture, beating constantly. Pour the whole mixture back into the pan and stir over medium heat for 5 minutes, or until the custard boils and thickens. Remove from the heat and add the vanilla. Cover the surface with plastic wrap and allow to cool, then fold in the whipped cream.

Spoon a third of the custard over the cherries and cake in the bowl. Top with more cake, syrup, cherries and custard. Continue layering, finishing with custard on top. Cover and refrigerate for 3-4 hours. Top with the extra whipped cream and almonds before serving.

PREPARATION TIME: 30 MINUTES +   COOKING TIME: 10 MINUTES

PETITS POTS AU CHOCOLAT

170 ml (5½ fl oz/⅔ cup) thick cream
½ vanilla bean, split lengthways
150 g (5½ oz/1 cup) chopped
dark chocolate
80 ml (2½ fl oz/⅓ cup) milk
2 egg yolks, at room temperature
55 g (2 oz/¼ cup) caster (superfine) sugar
whipped cream, to serve
unsweetened cocoa powder, to serve

SERVES 8

Lightly brush eight 80 ml (2½ fl oz/⅓ cup) ramekins with melted butter and put them in a roasting tin. Preheat the oven to 140°C (275°F/Gas 1). Heat the cream in a small pan with the vanilla bean until the cream is warm. Leave to infuse for 10 minutes then scrape the seeds out of the vanilla bean into the cream, and discard the empty bean.

Mix the chocolate and milk together in a saucepan. Stir constantly over low heat until the chocolate has just melted.

Place the egg yolks in a bowl and slowly whisk in the sugar. Continue whisking until the sugar has dissolved and the mixture is light and creamy. Add the vanilla cream and the melted chocolate to the beaten egg yolks and mix well.

Pour into the ramekins, filling approximately two-thirds of the way up. Pour enough boiling water into the roasting tin to come halfway up the sides of the ramekins. Bake for 45 minutes, or until the chocolate pots have puffed up slightly and feel spongy.

Remove from the roasting tin and set aside to cool completely. Cover with plastic wrap and refrigerate for 6 hours before serving. Serve with a dollop of cream and a sprinkle of sifted cocoa.

PREPARATION TIME: 20 MINUTES   COOKING TIME: 1 HOUR

CHOCOLATE LIQUEUR FRAPPE

260 g (9¼ oz/2 cups) ice cubes
125 ml (4 fl oz/½ cup) milk
60ml (2 fl oz/¼ cup) cream
2 tablespoons Frangelico
40 g (1½ oz/⅓ cup) icing
(confectioners') sugar
2 tablespoons unsweetened cocoa
powder, plus extra, to dust

SERVES 2

Put the ice, milk, cream, Frangelico, icing sugar and cocoa in a blender. Blend until thick and creamy. Pour into tall glasses, dust with extra cocoa and serve.

PREPARATION TIME: 5 MINUTES   COOKING TIME: NIL

CHOCOLATE AFFOGATO

1 litre (35 fl oz/4 cups) milk
285 g (10 oz/1¼ cups) caster
(superfine) sugar
½ teaspoon vanilla extract
140 g (5 oz) grated dark chocolate
6 small cups of espresso or very strong
coffee, freshly made
6 shots Frangelico

SERVES 6

Put the milk, sugar and vanilla in a saucepan over medium heat. Stir constantly for a few minutes, or until the sugar has dissolved and the milk is just about to boil.

Remove from the heat and stir in the chocolate. Continue to stir until the chocolate has melted and the mixture is smooth. Allow to cool slightly, then refrigerate until cold.

Transfer to an ice-cream machine and freeze according to the manufacturer's instructions. Alternatively, transfer to a shallow metal tray and freeze, whisking every couple of hours, until the gelato is frozen and creamy in texture. Freeze for about 5 hours, or overnight.

Scoop small balls of gelato out of the container and put them into six coffee cups or heatproof glasses, then put the cups in the freezer briefly while you make the coffee.

Serve the gelato with the coffee and Frangelico poured over it.

PREPARATION TIME: 15 MINUTES +   COOKING TIME: 5 MINUTES

Chocolate liqueur frappé

CHOCOLATE PANNA COTTA WITH POACHED RAISINS

300 ml (10½ fl oz) cream
185 ml (6 fl oz/¾ cup) milk
2 tablespoons caster (superfine) sugar
150 g (5½ oz) finely chopped milk chocolate
2 teaspoons powdered gelatine

POACHED RAISINS
125 g (4½ oz/1 cup) raisins
60 ml (2 fl oz/¼ cup) Pedro Ximenez, or other sweet sherry

SERVES 6

Mix together the cream, milk and sugar in a small saucepan. Stir over medium heat until the sugar dissolves. Bring to a simmer, then remove from the heat and add the chocolate. Stir until the chocolate melts and is well combined.

Place 2 teaspoons boiling water in a heatproof bowl. Sprinkle the gelatine over and use a fork to stir until the gelatine dissolves. Set aside for 1 minute, or until the liquid is clear. Add to the hot chocolate mixture and mix well. Strain into a jug. Cover and place in the fridge, stirring occasionally, for 1 hour or until cooled to room temperature.

Very lightly brush six 125 ml (4 fl oz/½ cup) ramekins with canola oil to grease. Place on a tray. Stir the cooled chocolate mixture and then divide it evenly among the ramekins. Place in the fridge for 6 hours, or until lightly set.

To make the poached raisins, combine the raisins and 2 tablespoons water in a small saucepan. Over low heat, gently simmer for 5 minutes, or until the raisins are soft and a light syrup has formed.

To serve, slide a palette knife down the side of each mould, one at a time, to create an air pocket, then turn out onto serving plates. Serve accompanied with the poached raisins.

PREPARATION TIME: 20 MINUTES   COOKING TIME: 10 MINUTES

CHOCOLATE BAVAROIS

250 g (7 oz/1²/3 cups) chopped dark chocolate
375 ml (13 fl oz/1¹/2 cups) milk
4 egg yolks, at room temperature
80 g (2³/4 oz/¹/3 cup) caster (superfine) sugar
1 tablespoon powdered gelatine
315 ml (10³/4 fl oz/1¹/4 cups) cream, for whipping
chocolate flakes, to serve

SERVES 6

Combine the chocolate and milk in a small saucepan. Stir over a low heat until the chocolate has melted and the milk just comes to the boil. Remove from the heat.

Beat the egg yolks and sugar until combined, then gradually add the hot chocolate milk, whisking until they are combined. Pour into a cleaned saucepan and over low heat, gently stir until the mixture is thick enough to coat the back of a wooden spoon. Do not allow it to boil. Remove from the heat.

Put 2 tablespoons water in a small heatproof bowl, sprinkle the gelatine in an even layer over the surface and leave to go spongy. Stir into the hot chocolate mixture until it dissolves. Refrigerate until cold but not set, stirring occasionally.

Beat the cream until soft peaks form, then fold into the chocolate mixture in two batches. Pour into six parfait glasses and refrigerate for several hours or overnight, or until set. Serve cold, topped with chocolate flakes.

PREPARATION TIME: 30 MINUTES   COOKING TIME: 10 MINUTES

CHOCOLATE MALAKOFF

100 ml (3½ fl oz) coffee liqueur
250 g (9 oz) small savoiardi (sponge finger biscuits)
50 g (1¾ oz/⅓ cup) chopped dark chocolate
125 g (4½ oz) unsalted butter, softened
145 g (6½ oz/⅔ cup) caster (superfine) sugar
½ teaspoon vanilla extract
125 g (4½ oz/1¼ cups) ground almonds
150 ml (5 fl oz) cream, whipped
150 g (5½ oz/1¼ cups) raspberries
unsweetened cocoa powder and icing (confectioners') sugar, to dust
extra raspberries, to serve

SERVES 6–8

Line a 1.5 litre (52 fl oz/6 cup) pudding basin (mould) with plastic wrap, allowing enough overhang to use as handles when unmoulding. Mix half the liqueur with 1 tablespoon water. Dip the smooth sides of the savoiardi briefly into the liquid and use them to neatly line the bottom and sides of the basin, placing the smooth sides of the biscuits inwards. Stand the biscuits upright around the side, and trim them to fit snugly.

To melt the chocolate, put the chocolate in a heatproof bowl. Half fill a saucepan with water, bring to the boil, then remove from the heat and sit the bowl over the pan (don't let the bowl touch the water or the chocolate will get too hot and seize). Stir frequently. Remove the bowl from the pan and stir in the remaining coffee liqueur, including any liquid left over from dipping the biscuits.

Cream the butter and sugar with electric beaters until pale and fluffy. Fold in the melted chocolate. Add the vanilla and ground almonds and fold in lightly but thoroughly. Fold in the whipped cream.

Spoon one-quarter of the mixture into the basin. Cover with one-third of the raspberries, then continue layering and finish with the remaining one-quarter of the mixture smoothed over the top. If you have any biscuits left, they can go on top. Cover and refrigerate overnight to set.

Use the plastic wrap to lever the pudding out of the basin (you can also run a knife around the inside of the basin to help loosen it), then invert it onto a serving plate. Remove the plastic wrap. Dust the top with cocoa, letting some of it drift down the side. Lightly dust icing sugar on top of the cocoa. Cut into slices and serve with extra raspberries.

PREPARATION TIME: 30 MINUTES   COOKING TIME: 5 MINUTES

CHOCOLATE CREME CARAMEL

185 g (6 oz/^{3}/4 cup) caster sugar

CUSTARD
4 egg yolks, at room temperature
60 g (2 oz/^{1}/4 cup) caster (superfine) sugar
315 ml (10^3/4 fl oz/1^1/4 cups) milk
185 ml (6 fl oz/^{3}/4 cup) cream
150 g (5^1/2 oz/1 cup) chopped
dark chocolate
whipped cream, to serve

MAKES 4

Preheat oven to 160°C (315°F/ Gas 2–3).

Combine the sugar and 185 ml (6 fl oz/^{3}/4 cup) water in a small saucepan. Stir over low heat without boiling until the sugar has dissolved. Bring to the boil and then reduce the heat. Simmer until the syrup just turns golden. Quickly pour the caramel into four 250 ml (9 fl oz/1 cup) ramekins. Allow to set.

To make the custard, whisk the egg yolks and sugar until just combined and slightly thickened. Combine the milk and cream in a saucepan. Bring to the boil, then remove from the heat. Add the chocolate to the milk and stir until melted. Gradually whisk into the egg mixture. Pour the custard through a fine strainer into a large jug. Pour the chocolate custard into the caramel-lined ramekins.

Place the ramekins in a roasting tin. Pour enough boiling water into the tin to come halfway up the sides of the ramekins. Bake for 45 minutes, or until the custard is just set (the custard will set more on standing). Remove from the water bath and set aside until cooled. Refrigerate overnight. Run a knife around the inside edge of each ramekin before turning out onto serving plates. Serve plain or with whipped cream and broken toffee pieces.

PREPARATION TIME: 25 MINUTES   COOKING TIME: 55 MINUTES

COFFEE CREMETS WITH CHOCOLATE SAUCE

250 g (9 oz/1 cup) cream cheese, softened
250 ml (9 fl oz/1 cup) thick (double/heavy) cream
80 ml (2½ oz/⅓ cup) very strong coffee
80 g (2¾ oz/⅓ cup) caster (superfine) sugar

CHOCOLATE SAUCE
100 g (3½ oz) dark chocolate
50 g (1¾ oz) unsalted butter

SERVES 4

Line four 100 ml (3½ fl oz) ramekins with muslin (cheesecloth), leaving enough muslin hanging over the side to wrap over the crémet.

Beat the cream cheese until smooth, then whisk in the cream. Add the coffee and sugar and mix well. Spoon into the ramekins and fold the muslin over the top.

Refrigerate for at least 1½ hours, then unwrap the muslin and turn the crémets out onto individual plates, carefully peeling the muslin off each one.

To make the chocolate sauce, gently melt the chocolate in a saucepan with the butter and 80 ml (2½ oz/⅓ cup) water. Stir well to make a shiny sauce, then allow the sauce to cool. Pour a little chocolate sauce over each crémet.

PREPARATION TIME: 20 MINUTES   COOKING TIME: 5 MINUTES

CHOCOLATE SWIRL PAVLOVA WITH DIPPED STRAWBERRIES

60 g (2¼ oz/heaped ¾ cup) chopped
dark chocolate
300 g (10½ oz) small to medium
strawberries
4 egg whites, at room temperature
pinch of cream of tartar
230 g (8 oz/1 cup) caster (superfine) sugar
250 ml (9 fl oz/1 cup) cream, for whipping
1 tablespoon strawberry or
raspberry liqueur
1 tablespoon icing (confectioners') sugar
3 tablespoons strawberry jam
1 tablespoon strawberry or raspberry
liqueur, extra

SERVES 8–10

Melt the chocolate in a heatproof bowl over a saucepan of simmering water. Don't let the base of the bowl touch the water or the chocolate will get too hot and seize. Dip eight of the strawberries partially into the chocolate, then put them on a sheet of baking paper and leave to set. Reserve the remaining chocolate. Hull the rest of the strawberries, then cut some in half lengthways, leaving the rest whole. Refrigerate until needed.

Preheat the oven to 150°C (300°F/Gas 2). Grease a baking tray and line with baking paper. Using electric beaters, whisk the egg whites until firm peaks form. Add the cream of tartar, then the sugar in a slow, steady stream, beating continuously. Continue to beat for about 5 minutes until the meringue is glossy and very thick.

Spoon one-third of the meringue onto the tray and spread it into a rough 23 cm (9 inch) round. With a spoon, drizzle over one-third of the melted chocolate, making swirls of chocolate in a marbled effect. Top with more meringue and chocolate drizzle, then repeat once more. Use a metal spatula to flatten slightly and smooth the surface.

Bake for 50 minutes, or until the edges and top of the meringue are dry. Turn the oven off, leave the door ajar and allow the meringue to cool fully.

Beat the cream, liqueur and icing sugar until thick. To serve, turn out onto a wire rack, peel off the baking paper and invert the pavlova onto a serving platter. Spread with the whipped cream. Arrange the whole and halved strawberries over the cream, interspersing them with the chocolate-coated strawberries.

Warm the strawberry jam, then pass it through a sieve and stir in the liqueur. Use a pastry brush to coat the strawberries with the extra jam mixture, until they look glossy. Cut the pavlova into thick wedges and serve immediately.

PREPARATION TIME: 30 MINUTES   COOKING TIME: 55 MINUTES

ZUCCOTTO

1 ready-made sponge cake
80 ml (2½ fl oz/⅓ cup) Kirsch
60 ml (2 fl oz/¼ cup) Cointreau
80 ml (2½ fl oz/⅓ cup) rum, cognac,
or Grand Marnier
500 ml (17 fl oz/2 cups) cream, for
whipping
90 g (3¼ oz) chopped dark roasted
almond chocolate
175 g (6 oz) finely chopped mixed
glacé (candied) fruit
100 g (3½ oz) dark chocolate, melted
70 g (2½ oz) hazelnuts, roasted
and chopped
unsweetened cocoa powder and icing
(confectioners') sugar, to decorate

SERVES 6–8

Line a 1.5 litre (52 fl oz/6 cup) pudding basin (mould) with damp muslin (cheesecloth). Cut the cake into curved pieces with a knife (you will need about 12 pieces). Work with one strip of cake at a time, brushing it with the combined liqueurs and arranging the pieces closely in the basin. Put the thin ends of the cake in the centre so the slices cover the base and side of the basin. Brush with the remaining liqueur to soak the cake. Put in the fridge to chill.

Beat the cream until stiff peaks form, then divide in half. Fold the almond chocolate and glacé fruit into one half and spread evenly over the cake in the basin, leaving a space in the centre.

Put the chocolate in a heatproof bowl. Half fill a saucepan with water, bring to the boil, then remove from the heat and sit the bowl over the pan (don't let the bowl touch the water or the chocolate will get too hot and seize). Stir occasionally until the chocolate melts. Allow to cool.

Fold the cooled melted chocolate and hazelnuts into the remaining cream and spoon into the centre cavity, packing it in firmly. Smooth the surface, cover and chill for 8 hours to allow the cream to firm slightly. Turn out onto a plate and dust with cocoa powder and icing sugar.

PREPARATION TIME: 1 HOUR   COOKING TIME: 10 MINUTES

CHOCOLATE TARTUFO

750 ml (26 fl oz/3 cups) milk
250 ml (9 fl oz/1 cup) cream
170 g (6 oz/¾ cup) caster
(superfine) sugar
125 g (4½ oz/1 cup) unsweetened
cocoa powder
80 g (2¾ oz/½ cup) finely chopped
dark chocolate
4 egg yolks, at room temperature
6 chocolate truffles
125 g (4½ oz/1 cup) finely grated
dark chocolate

MAKES 6

Put the milk, cream and half the sugar in a saucepan over medium heat. Stir constantly for 5 minutes, or until the sugar has dissolved and the mixture is just about to boil. Remove from the heat. Whisk in the cocoa and finely chopped chocolate.

Whisk the egg yolks and remaining sugar. Whisk in 60 ml (2 fl oz/¼ cup) of the hot chocolate mixture until smooth. Whisk in the remaining chocolate mixture, then pour into a saucepan and stir constantly over low heat for 10 minutes, or until the mixture thickens and coats the back of the spoon. Do not allow it to boil. Set aside to cool slightly, then put in the fridge to chill.

Transfer to an ice-cream machine and freeze according to the manufacturer's instructions. Alternatively, transfer to a shallow metal tray and freeze, whisking every couple of hours until frozen and creamy.

To assemble the tartufos, line twelve 125 ml (4 fl oz/½ cup) semi-circular ramekins with plastic wrap. Spoon in the ice-cream to come about 5 mm (¼ inch) from the top.

Sit a chocolate truffle in the centre of each of six ramekins, gently pushing them into the ice cream, but leaving the top of the truffles exposed. Freeze all the tartufos for 2 hours.

Carefully lift out the ice-cream ramekins without the truffles. Join them to the truffle-centred ice-cream, still in their ramekins, to make six balls.

Freeze for a further 1–2 hours, then carefully remove the tartufo balls from the ramekins. Roll each ball in grated chocolate and serve.

PREPARATION TIME: 30 MINUTES +   COOKING TIME: 15 MINUTES

CHOCOLATE AND CHESTNUT MARQUIS LOAF

125 g (4½ oz/heaped ¾ cup) chopped dark chocolate
110 g (3¾ oz) tinned sweetened chestnut purée
1 tablespoon brandy
50 g (1¾ oz) unsalted butter, softened
2 tablespoons unsweetened cocoa powder
3 tablespoons caster (superfine) sugar
2 egg yolks, at room temperature
1 teaspoon powdered gelatine
170 ml (5½ fl oz/⅔ cup) cream, for whipping
raspberries, to serve
icing (confectioners') sugar, to dust

SERVES 10–12

Line a 6 x 17 cm (2½ x 6½ inch) loaf (bar) tin with plastic wrap. Leave some overhang to assist with turning out. Melt the chocolate in a small heatproof bowl over a saucepan of simmering water. Don't let the base of the bowl touch the water or the chocolate will get too hot and seize. Stir frequently. Remove from the heat and stir in the chestnut purée and brandy. Allow to cool.

Using electric beaters, beat the butter, cocoa and half the sugar until creamy. In a separate small bowl, using electric beaters, beat the egg yolks and remaining sugar until creamy.

Put the gelatine in a small bowl with 2 teaspoons water. Set over a basin of hot water to dissolve the gelatine. In another bowl, beat the cream until firm peaks form, then set aside.

Using electric beaters, beat the cooled chocolate and chestnut mixture into the butter and cocoa mixture until smooth. Fold in the egg and gelatine, then fold in the beaten cream. Pour into the tin. Cover with the overlapping plastic and refrigerate for several hours, or overnight.

To serve, remove the marquis from the tin with the aid of the plastic wrap. Cut into thick slices while cold and put onto serving plates. Dust the raspberries with icing sugar and serve to the side.

PREPARATION TIME: 30 MINUTES   COOKING TIME: 5 MINUTES

CHOCOLATE MERINGUE TOWER

8 egg whites, at room temperature
310 g (11 oz/1⅓ cups) caster (superfine) sugar
½ teaspoon vanilla extract
30 g (1 oz/¼ cup) plain (all-purpose) flour, sifted
250 g (9 oz/1⅓ cups) ground almonds
300 g (10½ oz/2 cups) chopped dark chocolate, melted
500 ml (17 fl oz/2 cups) cream, whipped
300 g (10½ oz) milk chocolate, melted
50 g (1¾ oz/⅓ cup) each extra chopped dark and milk chocolate, melted, to decorate

SERVES 8–10

Preheat the oven to 120°C (235°F/Gas 1–2). Beat the egg whites until stiff peaks form. Gradually beat in 145 g (5 oz/⅔ cup) of the sugar until the meringue is stiff and glossy. Beat in the vanilla. Combine the remaining sugar, flour and ground almonds, then gently fold into the meringue.

Draw four circles on pieces of baking paper, each circle about 20 cm (8 inch) in diameter, and place on the baking trays. Spread the meringue evenly into each circle. Bake for 1 hour (you may have to make and cook the meringues in two batches). Cool the meringues completely and then peel off the paper.

Spread the top of the meringue with a quarter of the melted dark chocolate and then a quarter of the whipped cream. Spread the underside of the remaining 3 meringues with the melted milk chocolate. Put one of these, milk chocolate side down, on top of the first meringue. Spread this with dark chocolate and cream and top with another meringue. Continue layering, ending with the meringue on top. Drizzle the extra melted chocolate over the top in a lattice pattern.

PREPARATION TIME: 1 HOUR 30 MINUTES   COOKING TIME: 1 HOUR

HOT AND SAUCY

CHOCOLATE BREAD AND BUTTER PUDDING

60 g (2¼ oz) unsalted butter
6 slices fruit loaf bread
125 ml (4 fl oz/½ cup) milk
500 ml (17 fl oz/2 cups) cream
115 g (4 oz/½ cup) caster
(superfine) sugar
100 g (3⅓ oz) chopped dark chocolate
4 eggs, at room temperature,
lightly beaten
90 g (3¼ oz/½ cup) dark choc bits
2 tablespoons golden syrup

SERVES 4-6

Preheat the oven to 160°C (315°F/Gas 2-3). Brush a 1 litre (35 fl oz/4 cup) baking dish with oil or melted butter.

Spread butter on the slices of bread and cut into diagonal quarters. Place in the dish in a single layer, overlapping the quarters.

Combine the milk, cream and sugar in a saucepan and stir over low heat until the sugar dissolves. Bring to the boil and remove from the heat. Add the chocolate and stir until melted and smooth. Cool slightly, then gradually whisk in the eggs.

Pour half of the custard over the bread. Stand 10 minutes, or until the bread absorbs most of the liquid. Pour over the remaining custard. Sprinkle with the chocolate bits and drizzle with golden syrup. Bake for 40-45 minutes, or until set and slightly puffed and golden. Serve warm.

PREPARATION TIME: 25 MINUTES   COOKING TIME: 50 MINUTES

CHOCOLATE RAVIOLI

FILLING
60 g (2¼ oz) chopped dark chocolate
30 g (1 oz) unsalted butter, cubed
2½ tablespoons cream

DOUGH
250 g (9 oz/2 cups) plain (all-purpose) flour
½ teaspoon baking powder
2 teaspoons caster (superfine) sugar
1 egg, at room temperature
100 ml (3½ fl oz) light olive oil
2½ tablespoons dry white wine

1 egg, lightly beaten
vegetable oil, for deep-frying
icing (confectioners') sugar, to dust
125 ml (4 fl oz/½ cup) maple syrup, to serve

MAKES 18

To make the filling, put the chocolate, butter and cream in a small bowl set over a saucepan of simmering water. Stir until the chocolate and butter have melted and the mixture is smooth and glossy. Remove the bowl from the pan, cool and refrigerate until solid.

To make the dough, put the flour, baking powder, sugar and ¼ teaspoon salt in a food processor and pulse until just combined. Mix together the egg, olive oil and wine in a jug. Gradually pour into the processor while the motor is running, then stop processing when the mixture starts to clump together. Transfer to a lightly floured surface and knead for 3–4 minutes, or until smooth and elastic. Cover with plastic wrap and refrigerate for 30 minutes.

Roll the dough out to a 2–3 mm (¹⁄16–⅛ inch) thickness. Cover with a tea towel and allow to rest while you shape the filling.

Using a teaspoon or a small melon baller, scoop out rounded teaspoonfuls of the chocolate filling. They don't need to be perfectly round, but in a solid lump. If the kitchen is hot, keep the balls in the refrigerator and take out a few at a time as needed. You will need to make 18 balls.

With a biscuit cutter, cut 8 cm (3¼ inch) rounds from the dough. Brush around the rims of a few rounds with a little beaten egg. Place a chocolate ball in the centre of each. Fold the dough over to encase it, forming a half-moon shape. Press the edges together firmly to seal. Put on a tray and refrigerate while you make the rest of the ravioli.

Half fill a saucepan with oil and heat to 180°C (350°F), or until a cube of bread dropped in the oil browns in 15 seconds. Fry the ravioli, a few at a time, for 1½ minutes, or until puffed and golden brown. Drain on paper towels, then dust liberally with icing sugar. Serve warm while the chocolate centre is still melted, accompanied with a small bowl of maple syrup for dipping.

PREPARATION TIME: 30 MINUTES   COOKING TIME: 15 MINUTES

WHITE CHOCOLATE AND RASPBERRY RIPPLE RICE PUDDING

120 g (4¼ oz/1 cup) raspberries
2 tablespoons icing (confectioners') sugar
2 tablespoons raspberry liqueur,
such as Framboise
30 g (1 oz) unsalted butter
125 g (4½ oz/⅔ cup) risotto rice
1 vanilla bean, split lengthways
800 ml (28 fl oz) milk
55 g (1¾ oz/¼ cup) caster (superfine)
sugar
1 teaspoon vanilla extract
100 g (3½ oz/⅔ cup) chopped
white chocolate

SERVES 4

Using a hand blender, purée the raspberries, icing sugar and liqueur.

Melt the butter in a saucepan. Add the rice and vanilla bean and stir until the rice is coated in butter. In a separate saucepan, bring the milk, sugar and vanilla almost to the boil.

Ladle a spoonful of the milk mixture into the rice and stir constantly until the liquid has been absorbed.

Repeat until all the milk has been added and the rice is tender. Remove the vanilla bean (it can be dried and used again).

Add the white chocolate and stir until melted. Set aside for 5 minutes, then spoon the rice pudding into bowls. Swirl the raspberry purée through the rice to create a ripple effect. Serve warm.

PREPARATION TIME: 15 MINUTES   COOKING TIME: 20 MINUTES

CHOCOLATE CROISSANT PUDDING

4 croissants, torn into pieces

125 g (4½ oz) chopped dark chocolate

4 eggs, at room temperature

55 g (2¼ oz/¼ cup) caster (superfine) sugar

250 ml (9 fl oz/1 cup) milk

250 ml (9 fl oz/1 cup) cream

3 teaspoons orange liqueur

3 teaspoons grated orange zest

80 ml (2½ fl oz/⅓ cup) orange juice

2 tablespoons roughly chopped hazelnuts

SERVES 6–8

Preheat the oven to 180°C (350°F/Gas 4). Grease a 20 cm (8 inch) round cake tin and line the base with baking paper. Put the croissant pieces and 100 g (3½ oz) of the chocolate into the tin.

Beat the eggs and sugar together until pale and creamy. In a saucepan, bring the milk, cream, liqueur and remaining chocolate almost to the boil. Stir to melt the chocolate, then remove the pan from the heat.

Gradually add this mixture to the egg mixture, stirring constantly. Stir in the orange zest and juice. Pour over the croissants, a little at a time, allowing the liquid to be fully absorbed before adding more.

Sprinkle the hazelnuts over the top and bake for 50 minutes, or until a skewer poked into the centre comes out clean. Cool in the tin for about 10 minutes, then turn out and invert onto a serving plate. Slice into thick wedges and serve.

PREPARATION TIME: 20 MINUTES   COOKING TIME: 1 HOUR

HOT MOCHA SOUFFLE

3 tablespoons caster (superfine) sugar
40 g (1½ oz) unsalted butter
2 tablespoons plain (all-purpose) flour
185 ml (6 fl oz/¾ cup) milk
1 tablespoon instant espresso-style
coffee powder
100 g (3½ oz/⅔ cup) dark chocolate,
melted
4 eggs, at room temperature, separated
icing (confectioners') sugar, to dust

SERVES 20

Preheat the oven to 180°C (350°F/Gas 4). Wrap a double thickness of baking paper around a 1.25 litre (44 fl oz/5 cup) soufflé dish extending 3 cm (1¼ inches) above the rim. Tie securely with string. Brush with oil or melted butter, sprinkle 1 tablespoon of the sugar into the dish, shake the dish to coat the base and side evenly, then shake out any excess.

Melt the butter in a saucepan, add the flour and stir over low heat for 2 minutes, or until lightly golden. Gradually add the milk and stir until smooth. Stir over medium heat until the mixture boils and thickens, then boil for another minute. Remove from the heat and transfer to a large bowl.

Put the chocolate in a heatproof bowl. Half fill a saucepan with water, bring to the boil, then remove from the heat and sit the bowl over the pan (don't let the bowl touch the water or the chocolate will get too hot and seize). Stir occasionally until the chocolate melts.

Dissolve the coffee in 1 tablespoon hot water, add to the milk mixture along with the remaining sugar, melted chocolate and egg yolks, then beat until smooth.

Beat the egg whites until stiff peaks form and then fold a little into the chocolate mixture to loosen it slightly. Gently fold in the remaining egg white, then spoon the mixture into the soufflé dish and bake for 40 minutes, or until well risen and just firm. Remove the collar, dust the soufflé with icing sugar and serve immediately.

PREPARATION TIME: 25 MINUTES   COOKING TIME: 45 MINUTES

CHOCOLATE FUDGE PUDDINGS

160 g (5½ oz) unsalted butter, softened
170 g (6 oz/¾ cup) caster
(superfine) sugar
100 g (3½ oz) chocolate, melted
and cooled
2 eggs, at room temperature
60 g (2¼ oz/½ cup) plain (all-purpose)
flour
125 g (4½ oz/1 cup) self-raising flour
30 g (1 oz/¼ cup) unsweetened
cocoa powder
1 teaspoon bicarbonate of soda (baking
soda)
125 ml (4 fl oz/½ cup) milk
whipped cream, to serve

SAUCE
60 g (2¼ oz) unsalted butter, chopped
115 g (4 oz) chocolate, chopped
125 ml (4 fl oz/½ cup) cream
1 teaspoon vanilla extract

SERVES 8

Preheat the oven to 180°C (350°F/Gas 4). Lightly grease eight 250 ml (9 fl oz/1 cup) ramekins with melted butter and line the bases with rounds of baking paper.

Beat the butter and sugar until light and creamy. Add the melted chocolate, beating well. Add the eggs one at a time, beating well after each addition.

Sift together the flours, cocoa, and bicarbonate of soda, then fold into the chocolate. Add the milk and fold through. Pour into the ramekins until they are half full.

Cover the ramekins with buttered foil and place in a roasting tin. Pour enough boiling water into the tin to come halfway up the sides of the ramekins. Bake for 35–40 minutes, or until a skewer poked into the centre of a pudding comes out clean.

To make the sauce, combine the butter, chocolate, cream and vanilla in a saucepan. Stir over low heat until the butter and chocolate have completely melted. Pour over the pudding and serve with whipped cream.

PREPARATION TIME: 20 MINUTES   COOKING TIME: 45 MINUTES

STEAMED CHOCOLATE AND PRUNE PUDDINGS

125 g (4½ oz) unsalted butter, softened
125 g (4½ oz/⅔ cup) soft brown sugar
3 eggs, at room temperature
125 g (4½ oz/1 cup) self-raising flour
40 g (1½ oz/⅓ cup) unsweetened cocoa powder
60 ml (2 fl oz/¼ cup) milk
150 g (5½ oz) chopped dark chocolate
125 g (4½ oz/½ cup) chopped pitted prunes
icing (confectioners') sugar, to dust

COGNAC CREAM
330 ml (11¼ fl oz/1⅓ cups) thick (double/heavy) cream
2 tablespoons icing (confectioners') sugar, sifted
2 tablespoons Cognac or brandy

SERVES 8

Preheat the oven to 180°C (350°F/Gas 4). Brush eight 185 ml (6 fl oz/¾ cup) ramekins with melted butter. Line the bases with rounds of baking paper.

Beat the butter and brown sugar with electric beaters until pale and creamy. Add the eggs one at a time, beating well after each addition. Sift together the flour and cocoa over the butter mixture and fold together. Fold in the milk, then fold in the chocolate and prunes until evenly combined.

Spoon the mixture into the ramekins and smooth the surface. Cover each pudding with a piece of buttered foil, folding the edges of the foil tightly around the rim of the ramekin. Place the ramekins in a roasting tin. Add enough boiling water to the tin to reach half way up the sides of the ramekins. Bake for 45–50 minutes, or until a skewer comes out clean when poked into the centre of a pudding.

Meanwhile, to make the cognac cream, combine the cream, icing sugar and Cognac. Cover and place in the fridge.

Stand the puddings in the ramekins for 5 minutes before turning out onto serving plates. Dust the puddings with icing sugar and serve with the cognac cream.

PREPARATION TIME: 20 MINUTES   COOKING TIME: 50 MINUTES

PEARS IN SPICED CHOCOLATE SYRUP

115 g (4 oz/½ cup) caster (superfine) sugar
30 g (1 oz/¼ cup) unsweetened cocoa powder, sifted
2 tablespoons golden syrup
1 star anise
1 cinnamon stick
½ teaspoon black peppercorns
4 firm ripe pears (such as beurre bosc)
vanilla ice cream or whipped cream, to serve

SERVES 4

Combine the sugar and cocoa in a saucepan. Gradually stir in 1 litre (35 fl oz/4 cups) water. Add the golden syrup, star anise, cinnamon stick and peppercorns. Stir over medium heat until the sugar and golden syrup dissolve. Bring to a simmer.

Meanwhile, remove the cores from the pears, leaving the stems intact. If necessary, trim the base of the pears slightly so they stand upright. Peel the pears.

Add the pears to the syrup and simmer gently, uncovered, turning occasionally, for 10–15 minutes, or until just tender when tested with a skewer.

Use a slotted spoon to transfer the pears to a plate. Cover with foil and set aside to keep warm. Bring the syrup to the boil and boil for 20 minutes, or until thick and reduced by about half. Serve the pears accompanied with the syrup and cream.

PREPARATION TIME: 25 MINUTES   COOKING TIME: 40 MINUTES

CHOCOLATE FRENCH TOAST

50 g (1³/₄ oz/¹/₃ cup) chopped
dark chocolate
four 1.5 cm (⁵/₈ inch) thick slices
day-old brioche
or 4 slices cob or cottage loaf
1 egg, at room temperature
1¹/₂ tablespoons cream
1¹/₂ tablespoons milk
1 tablespoon caster (superfine) sugar
¹/₂ teaspoon vanilla extract
¹/₄ teaspoon ground cinnamon
20 g (³/₄ oz) unsalted butter
icing (confectioners') sugar, to dust

SERVES 2

Place the chocolate in a small heatproof bowl over a saucepan of simmering water. Don't let the bowl touch the water or the chocolate will get too hot and seize. Stir frequently until the chocolate just melts and the mixture is smooth. Remove the bowl from the saucepan.

Spread two slices of brioche (or cob or cottage loaf) with the melted chocolate and sandwich together, repeat with the remaining slices.

Use a fork to whisk the egg, cream, milk, sugar, vanilla and cinnamon in a wide bowl.

Place the sandwiches into the egg mixture, allowing the bread to soak it up (allow about 30 seconds each side). Meanwhile, melt the butter in a frying pan over medium heat.

When the butter is sizzling, remove the sandwiches, allowing any excess egg mixture to drain off, and add to the pan. Cook for 2 minutes each side, or until well browned.

Cut the sandwiches in half and serve, dusted with icing sugar.

PREPARATION TIME: 20 MINUTES   COOKING TIME: 10 MINUTES

CHOCOLATE CREPES WITH GRAND MARNIER SAUCE

2 eggs, at room temperature
2 tablespoons caster (superfine) sugar
60 g (2¼ oz/½ cup) plain (all-purpose) flour
1 tablespoon unsweetened cocoa powder
250 ml (9 fl oz/1 cup) milk
3 oranges
125 g (4½ oz/½ cup) sour cream or crème fraîche
75 g (2½ oz/½ cup) grated white chocolate
250 g (9 oz) blueberries

SAUCE
180 g (6½ oz/1¼ cups) chopped dark chocolate
185 ml (6 fl oz/¾ cup) cream
2–3 tablespoons Grand Marnier

MAKES 8–10

Whisk the eggs and sugar in a large jug. Gradually whisk in the sifted flour and cocoa, alternately with the milk, until the batter is free of lumps. Cover with plastic wrap and set aside for 30 minutes.

Cut a 1 cm (½ inch) slice from the ends of each orange. Cut the skin away in a circular motion, cutting only deep enough to remove all the white membrane and skin. Cut the flesh into segments between each membrane. (Do this over a bowl to catch any juice.) Place the segments in the bowl with the juice. Cover with plastic wrap and refrigerate.

Heat a 20 cm (8 inch) frying pan over medium heat. Brush lightly with a little melted butter. Pour 2–3 tablespoons of crepe batter into the pan and swirl evenly over the base. Cook over medium heat for 1 minute or until the underside is cooked. Turn the crepe over and cook the other side. Transfer the crepe to a plate and cover with a tea towel to keep warm. Continue making crepes until you use all the batter. (This mixture should make 8–10 crepes, depending on their thickness.)

To make the sauce, drain the oranges, reserving the juice. Put the juice in a saucepan with the chocolate, cream and Grand Marnier. Stir over low heat until the chocolate has melted and the mixture is smooth.

To assemble the crepes, place 1 heaped teaspoon of sour cream on a quarter of each crepe. Sprinkle with the grated white chocolate. Fold the crepe in half, and in half again to make a wedge shape. Place two crepes on each serving plate. Spoon the warm sauce over the crepes and serve with orange segments and blueberries.

PREPARATION TIME: 40 MINUTES +   COOKING TIME: 20 MINUTES

MOLTEN CHOCOLATE PUDDINGS

200 g (7 oz/1⅓ cups) chopped dark chocolate

100 g (3½ oz) unsalted butter, cubed

2 eggs, at room temperature

2 egg yolks, at room temperature

55 g (2 oz/¼ cup) caster (superfine) sugar

2 tablespoons plain (all-purpose) flour, sifted

unsweetened cocoa powder, to dust

MALT CREAM

200 ml (7 fl oz) cream, for whipping

45 g (1½ oz/⅓ cup) malted milk powder

1 tablespoon icing (confectioners') sugar, sifted

SERVES 6

Preheat the oven to 180°C (350°F/Gas 4). Brush six 185 ml (6 fl oz/¾ cup) ramekins with melted butter. Place on a baking tray.

Combine the chocolate and butter in a small saucepan over low heat. Stir frequently until the chocolate and butter have melted and the mixture is smooth. Remove from the heat.

Beat the whole eggs, egg yolks and sugar with electric beaters until thick and pale. Add the chocolate mixture and flour and use a large metal spoon or spatula to fold in until evenly combined.

Divide the mixture evenly among the ramekins. Bake for 12 minutes, or until the puddings have risen almost to the top of the ramekins (they will still look slightly underdone).

Meanwhile, to make the malt cream, whisk together the cream, malted milk powder and icing sugar until soft peaks form. Cover and place in the fridge.

To serve, turn the puddings out onto serving plates . Dust with the cocoa powder and serve with the malt cream.

PREPARATION TIME: 20 MINUTES   COOKING TIME: 20 MINUTES

CHOCOLATE SOUFFLES

180 g (6½ oz/1¼ cups) chopped dark
chocolate
5 eggs, at room temperature, separated
55 g (2 oz/¼ cup) caster (superfine) sugar
2 egg whites, extra
icing (confectioners') sugar, for dusting

SERVES 6

Preheat the oven to 200°C (400°F/Gas 6) and put a baking tray into the oven to warm.

Wrap a double layer of baking paper around the outside of six 250 ml (9 fl oz/1 cup) ramekins to come about 3 cm (1¼ inches) above the rim, and secure with string. This encourages the soufflé to rise well. Brush the insides of the ramekins with melted butter and sprinkle with a little caster sugar, shaking to coat evenly and tipping out any excess. This layer of butter and sugar helps the soufflé to grip the sides and rise as it cooks.

Place the chocolate in a heatproof bowl set over a saucepan of simmering water. Don't let the bowl touch the water, or the chocolate will get too hot and seize. Stir until the chocolate is melted and smooth, then remove from the heat. Stir in the egg yolks and caster sugar.

Beat the 7 egg whites until stiff peaks form. Gently fold one-third of the egg whites into the chocolate mixture to loosen it. Then, using a metal spoon, fold in the remaining egg whites until just combined.

Spoon the mixture into the ramekins and run your thumb or a blunt knife around the inside rim of the dish and the edge of the mixture. This ridge helps the soufflé to rise evenly. Place on the heated baking tray and bake for 12–15 minutes, or until well risen and just set. Do not open the oven door while the soufflés are baking.

Cut the string and remove the paper collars. Serve immediately, lightly dusted with sifted icing sugar.

PREPARATION TIME: 20 MINUTES   COOKING TIME: 20 MINUTES

CHOCOLATE AND CINNAMON SELF-SAUCING PUDDINGS

50 g (1³/4 oz/¹/3 cup) chopped dark chocolate

60 g (2¹/4 oz) unsalted butter, cubed

2 tablespoons unsweetened cocoa powder, sifted

170 ml (5¹/4 fl oz/²/3 cup) milk

125 g (4¹/2 oz/1 cup) self-raising flour

115 g (4 oz/¹/2 cup) caster (superfine) sugar

80 g (2³/4 oz/¹/3 cup firmly packed) soft brown sugar

1 egg, at room temperature, lightly beaten

CINNAMON SAUCE

1¹/2 teaspoons ground cinnamon

50 g (1³/4 oz) unsalted butter, cubed

60 g (2¹/4 oz/¹/4 cup firmly packed) soft brown sugar

30 g (1 oz/¹/4 cup) unsweetened cocoa powder, sifted

SERVES 4

Preheat the oven to 180°C (350°F/Gas 4). Grease four 250 ml (9 fl oz/ 1 cup) ramekins.

Combine the chocolate, butter, cocoa and milk in a saucepan. Stir over low heat until the chocolate has melted. Remove from the heat.

Sift the flour into a large bowl and stir in the sugars. Add to the chocolate mixture with the egg and mix well. Spoon into the ramekins, put on a baking tray and set aside while you make the sauce.

To make the cinnamon sauce, combine the cinnamon, butter, brown sugar, cocoa and 375 ml (13 fl oz/1¹/2 cups) water in a saucepan. Stir over low heat until combined. Carefully pour the sauce onto the puddings over the back of a spoon. Bake for 40 minutes, or until firm. Serve warm with thick cream or ice cream.

PREPARATION TIME: 20 MINUTES   COOKING TIME: 50 MINUTES

CHOCOLATE MINT SELF-SAUCING PUDDING

185 ml (6 fl oz/³/₄ cup) milk

115 g (4 oz/¹/₂ cup) caster (superfine) sugar

60 g (2¹/₄ oz) unsalted butter, melted

1 egg, at room temperature

125 g (4¹/₂ oz/1 cup) self-raising flour

40 g (1¹/₂ oz/¹/₃ cup) unsweetened cocoa powder

125 g (4¹/₂ oz) roughly chopped mint-flavoured dark chocolate

230 g (8 oz/1 cup firmly packed) soft brown sugar

ice cream, to serve

SERVES 6

Preheat the oven to 180°C (350°F/Gas 4). Grease a 1.5 litre (52 fl oz/ 6 cup) ovenproof dish.

Whisk together the milk, sugar, butter and egg. Sift the flour and half the cocoa powder onto the milk mixture, add the chocolate and stir. Pour into the dish. Put the brown sugar and remaining cocoa into a bowl and stir in 250 ml (9 fl oz/1 cup) boiling water. Carefully pour this over the pudding mixture.

Bake for 40–45 minutes, or until the pudding is cooked and firm to touch. Spoon over the sauce and serve hot or warm with ice cream.

PREPARATION TIME: 15 MINUTES   COOKING TIME: 45 MINUTES

WAFFLES WITH HOT CHOCOLATE SAUCE

250 g (9 oz/2 cups) self-raising flour

1 teaspoon bicarbonate of soda (baking soda)

2 teaspoons sugar

2 eggs, at room temperature

90 g (3¹/₄ oz) unsalted butter, melted

440 ml (15 fl oz/1³/₄ cups) buttermilk

HOT CHOCOLATE SAUCE

50 g (1³/₄ oz) unsalted butter

200 g (6¹/₂ oz/1¹/₃ cups) chopped dark chocolate

125 ml (4 fl oz/¹/₂ cup) cream

1 tablespoon golden syrup

SERVES 8

Sift the flour, bicarbonate of soda, sugar and a pinch of salt and make a well in the centre. Whisk the eggs, melted butter and the buttermilk in a jug and gradually pour into the well, whisking until the batter is just smooth. Set aside for 10 minutes. Preheat the waffle iron.

To make the chocolate sauce, put the butter, chopped chocolate, cream and golden syrup in a saucepan and stir over low heat until smooth. Remove from the heat and keep warm.

Grease the waffle iron. Pour 125 ml (4 fl oz/¹/₂ cup) batter into the centre and spread almost to the corners of the grid. Cook for 2 minutes, or until golden and crisp. Serve with vanilla ice cream and hot chocolate sauce.

PREPARATION TIME: 20 MINUTES   COOKING TIME: 25 MINUTES

CHOCOLATE AND ALMOND PEAR PUDDINGS

115 g (4 oz/⅓ cup) golden syrup

8 tinned pear halves in natural juice, drained

60 g (2¼ oz/½ cup) plain (all-purpose) flour

30 g (1 oz/¼ cup) unsweetened cocoa powder

2 teaspoons baking powder

1 teaspoon ground allspice (optional)

55 g (2 oz/½ cup) ground almonds

3 eggs, at room temperature

165 g (5¾ oz/¾ cup firmly packed) soft brown sugar

60 ml (2 fl oz/¼ cup) milk

115 g (4 oz/⅓ cup) golden syrup, extra warmed slightly, to serve

vanilla ice cream or cream, to serve

Preheat the oven to 180°C (350°F/Gas 4). Brush eight holes of a 12-hole muffin tray with melted butter to grease, and line the base with rounds of baking paper. Divide the golden syrup evenly among the eight muffin holes to cover the bases. Place a pear half, cut side down, in each.

Sift together the flour, cocoa, baking powder and allspice, if using. Stir in the ground almonds.

Use an electric beater with a whisk attachment to whisk the eggs and sugar until thick and pale. Pour in the milk, add the flour mixture and use a metal spoon to fold together.

Spoon the cake mixture evenly over the pears. Bake for 25 minutes, or until a skewer comes out clean when poked into the centre of a pudding. Stand for 3 minutes before turning out onto a wire rack. Immediately remove the baking paper and transfer the puddings to serving plates. Drizzle with extra golden syrup and serve with cream or ice cream.

SERVES 8   PREPARATION TIME: 20 MINUTES   COOKING TIME: 25 MINUTES

DARK CHOCOLATE PUDDINGS WITH COFFEE LIQUEUR SAUCE

125 g (4½ oz) unsalted butter, softened

115 g (4 oz/½ cup) caster (superfine) sugar

1 teaspoon vanilla extract

2 eggs, at room temperature

125 g (4½ oz/1 cup) plain (all-purpose) flour

60 g (2¼ oz/½ cup) unsweetened cocoa powder

2 teaspoons baking powder

100 ml (3½ fl oz) milk

60 g (2¼ oz/⅓ cup) finely chopped dark chocolate

35 g (1¼ oz/¼ cup) roasted hazelnuts, skinned and chopped

cream, to serve

fresh berries, to serve

COFFEE LIQUEUR MOCHA SAUCE

30 g (1 oz) butter

80 g (2¾ oz/½ cup) chopped dark chocolate

170 ml (5½ fl oz/⅔ cup) cream

1 teaspoon instant coffee granules

2 tablespoons coffee-flavoured liqueur (such as Kahlùa)

SERVES 6

Preheat the oven to 180°C (350°F/Gas 4). Grease six 250 ml (9 fl oz/ 1 cup) ramekins and put them on a baking tray.

Beat the butter, sugar and vanilla with electric beaters for 2 minutes until thick and creamy. Add the eggs one at a time, beating well after each addition. Fold in the sifted flour, cocoa and baking powder with a metal spoon, adding the milk alternately with the flour mixture. Stir in the chocolate. Spoon into the ramekins and smooth the surface.

Bake for about 15 minutes, or until risen and just firm to the touch. Leave for 5 minutes, then run a small flat-bladed knife between the puddings and the ramekins and turn them out onto a wire rack.

To make the sauce, combine the butter, chocolate, cream and coffee granules in a saucepan over low heat. Stir until the chocolate has melted and the mixture is smooth. Remove from the heat and stir in the liqueur. Keep warm.

To serve, put the hot puddings on serving plates, pour over some of the sauce, scatter over a few chopped hazelnuts and serve with cream and berries.

PREPARATION TIME: 15 MINUTES   COOKING TIME: 20 MINUTES

CHOCOLATE CHIP PANCAKES WITH HOT FUDGE SAUCE

250 g (9 oz/2 cups) self-raising flour

2 tablespoons unsweetened cocoa powder

1 teaspoon bicarbonate of soda (baking soda)

55 g (2 oz/¼ cup) caster (superfine) sugar

130 g (4½ oz/¾ cup) dark chocolate bits

250 ml (9 fl oz/1 cup) milk

250 ml (9 fl oz/1 cup) cream

2 eggs, at room temperature, lightly beaten

30 g (1 oz) unsalted butter, melted

3 egg whites, at room temperature

whipped cream or ice cream, to serve

icing (confectioners') sugar, to dust

HOT FUDGE SAUCE

150 g (5½ oz/1 cup) chopped dark chocolate

30 g (1 oz) unsalted butter

2 tablespoons light corn syrup

95 g (3¼ oz/½ cup) soft brown sugar

125 ml (4 fl oz/½ cup) cream

MAKES 16

Sift the flour, cocoa and bicarbonate of soda into a bowl. Stir in the sugar and chocolate bits and make a well in the centre. Whisk the milk, cream, eggs and melted butter in a jug, then gradually pour into the well and stir until just combined. Cover and set aside for 15 minutes.

Beat the egg whites until soft peaks form. Using a large metal spoon, stir a heaped tablespoon of the beaten egg white into the batter to loosen it up, then lightly fold in the remaining egg white.

Heat a frying pan and brush lightly with melted butter or oil. Pour 60 ml (2 fl oz/¼ cup) of batter into the pan and cook over medium heat until the underside is browned.

Flip the pancake over and cook the other side. Transfer to a plate, and cover with a tea towel while cooking the remaining batter. Stack between sheets of baking paper to prevent the pancakes sticking together.

To make the hot fudge sauce, put all the ingredients in a saucepan and stir over low heat until melted and smooth. Dust the pancakes with icing sugar and serve warm with whipped cream or ice cream and drizzled with hot fudge sauce.

PREPARATION TIME: 35 MINUTES   COOKING TIME: 30 MINUTES

CHOCOLATE RUM FONDUE

250 g (9 oz/1²⁄₃ cups) chopped dark chocolate

125 ml (4 fl oz/½ cup) cream

1–2 tablespoons rum

1 mandarin, tangerine or small orange, peeled, divided into segments

2 figs, quartered lengthways

250 g (9 oz/1²⁄₃ cups) strawberries, hulled

250 g (9 oz/2³⁄₄ cups) white marshmallows

SERVES 6

Melt the chocolate and cream in a heatproof bowl over a saucepan of simmering water. Don't let the bowl touch the water or the chocolate will get too hot and seize. Stir until smooth, remove the bowl from the heat and stir in the rum, to taste. Pour while still warm into the fondue pot.

Arrange the fruit and marshmallows on a serving platter. Serve with forks to dip the fruit into the chocolate fondue.

PREPARATION TIME: 15 MINUTES   COOKING TIME: 10 MINUTES

WHITE CHOCOLATE FONDUE WITH FRUIT

125 ml (4 fl oz/½ cup) light corn syrup

170 ml (5½ fl oz/²⁄₃ cup) thick (double/heavy) cream

60 ml (2 fl oz/¼ cup) Cointreau or orange-flavoured liqueur

250 g (9 oz/1²⁄₃ cups) chopped white chocolate

marshmallows and fresh fruit such as sliced peaches, strawberries and cherries

SERVES 6–8

Combine the corn syrup and cream in a small saucepan or fondue. Bring to the boil, then remove from the heat.

Add the liqueur and white chocolate and stir until melted. Transfer to a fondue pot. Serve with marshmallows and fresh fruit.

PREPARATION TIME: 15 MINUTES   COOKING TIME: 10 MINUTES

THE ULTIMATE HOT CHOCOLATE

60 g (2½ oz) chopped dark chocolate
500 ml (17 fl oz/2 cups) milk, warmed
marshmallows, to serve

MAKES 2

Put the chocolate in a saucepan. Add 2 tablespoons water and stir over low heat until the chocolate has melted. Gradually pour in the milk, whisking until smooth and slightly frothy. Heat without boiling. Pour into mugs and float one or two marshmallows on top.

PREPARATION TIME: 5 MINUTES   COOKING TIME: 5 MINUTES

COCOA-SCENTED TEA

50 g (1¾ oz/⅓ cup) Callebaut cocoa nibs
(100% roasted cocoa nibs)
2 tablespoons English Breakfast
tea leaves
2 vanilla beans, finely chopped

MAKES ENOUGH FOR 12 CUPS OF TEA

Combine the cocoa nibs, tea leaves and vanilla beans in a glass jar. Seal and store for at least 2 weeks to infuse before using.

Place 2 teaspoons of cocoa-scented tea in a tea ball. Place the tea ball in a 250 ml (9 fl oz/1 cup) heatproof glass. Add 185 ml (6 fl oz/¾ cup) of just boiling water and set aside to infuse for 5 minutes. Remove the tea ball. Add 1 teaspoon of sugar (or to taste) and milk, if desired. Serve immediately.

PREPARATION TIME: 10 MINUTES   COOKING TIME: NIL

The ultimate hot chocolate

CRISPY CRUNCHY

CHOCOLATE CHIP COOKIES

185 g (6½ oz/1½ cups) plain (all-purpose) flour
90 g (3¼ oz/¾ cup) unsweetened cocoa powder
280 g (10 oz/1½ cups) soft brown sugar
180 g (6½ oz) unsalted butter, cubed
150 g (5 oz/1 cup) chopped dark chocolate
3 eggs, at room temperature, lightly beaten
265 g (9¼ oz/1½ cups) chocolate bits

MAKES 40

Preheat the oven to 180°C (350°F/Gas 4). Line two baking trays with baking paper.

Sift the flour and cocoa into a large bowl, add the sugar and make a well in the centre.

Put the butter and chocolate in a small heatproof bowl. Bring a saucepan of water to the boil, then remove the pan from the heat. Sit the bowl over the saucepan. Stir occasionally until the chocolate and butter have melted and are smooth.

Add the butter and chocolate mixture and the eggs to the dry ingredients. Mix well with a wooden spoon, but do not overmix. Stir in the chocolate bits. Drop tablespoons of the mixture onto the trays, allowing room for spreading. Bake for 7–10 minutes, or until firm to touch. Cool on the trays for 5 minutes before transferring to a wire rack to cool completely.

PREPARATION TIME: 20 MINUTES   COOKING TIME: 15 MINUTES

TOLLHOUSE COOKIES

180 g (6½ oz) unsalted butter, cubed and softened
140 g (5 oz/¾ cup) soft brown sugar
110 g (3¾ oz/½ cup) sugar
2 eggs, at room temperature, lightly beaten
1 teaspoon vanilla extract
280 g (10 oz/2¼ cups) plain (all-purpose) flour
1 teaspoon bicarbonate of soda (baking soda)
350 g (12 oz/2 cups) dark chocolate bits
100 g (3½ oz/1 cup) pecans, roughly chopped

MAKES 40

Preheat the oven to 190°C (375°F/Gas 5). Line two baking trays with baking paper.

Cream the butter and sugars with electric beaters until light and fluffy. Gradually add the egg, beating well after each addition. Stir in the vanilla, then the sifted flour and bicarbonate of soda until just combined. Mix in the chocolate bits and pecans.

Drop tablespoons of mixture onto the trays, leaving room for spreading. Bake the cookies for 8–10 minutes, or until lightly golden. Cool slightly on the trays before transferring to a wire rack to cool completely. When completely cold, store in an airtight container.

PREPARATION TIME: 20 MINUTES   COOKING TIME: 10 MINUTES

CRACKLE COOKIES

125 g (4½ oz) unsalted butter, cubed and softened
375 g (13 oz/2 cups) soft brown sugar
1 teaspoon vanilla extract
2 eggs, at room temperature
60 g (2¼ oz) dark chocolate, melted
80 ml (2½ fl oz/⅓ cup) milk
340 g (12 oz/2¾ cups) plain (all-purpose) flour
2 tablespoons unsweetened cocoa powder
2 teaspoons baking powder
¼ teaspoon ground allspice
85 g (3 oz/⅔ cup) chopped pecans
icing (confectioners') sugar, to coat

MAKES 60

Lightly grease two baking trays. Cream the butter, sugar and vanilla until light and creamy. Beat in the eggs one at a time, beating well after each addition. Stir the melted chocolate and milk into the butter mixture.

Sift the flour, cocoa, baking powder, allspice and a pinch of salt into the butter mixture and mix well. Stir the pecans through. Refrigerate for at least 3 hours or overnight.

Preheat the oven to 180°C (350°F/Gas 4). Roll tablespoons of the mixture into balls and roll each in the icing sugar to coat.

Place on the trays, allowing room for spreading. Bake for 20–25 minutes, or until lightly browned. Leave for 3–4 minutes, then cool on a wire rack.

PREPARATION TIME: 15 MINUTES +   COOKING TIME: 25 MINUTES

DRIED FRUIT AND CHOCOLATE PILLOWS

CREAM CHEESE PASTRY

90 g (3¼ oz/⅓ cup) cream cheese, softened

55 g (2¼ oz/¼ cup) caster (superfine) sugar

1 egg yolk, at room temperature

60 ml (2 fl oz/¼ cup) milk

185 g (6½ oz/1½ cups) plain (all-purpose) flour

1 teaspoon baking powder

1 egg white, at room temperature, to glaze

DRIED FRUIT FILLING

60 g (2¼ oz/⅓ cup) chopped dried figs

95 g (3¼ oz/½ cup) chopped dried apricots

60 g (2¼ oz/½ cup) raisins, chopped

60 g (2¼ oz) chopped dark chocolate

½ teaspoon grated lemon zest

80 g (2¾ oz/¼ cup) clear honey

large pinch ground allspice

large pinch ground cinnamon

MAKES 24

To make the cream cheese pastry, beat the cheese and sugar until fluffy. Beat in the egg yolk and milk, then sift in the flour, a pinch of salt and the baking powder and form into a smooth dough. Cover with plastic wrap and refrigerate for 2 hours.

To make the dried fruit filling, put all the ingredients in a food processor and pulse until finely chopped.

Preheat the oven to 180°C (350°F/Gas 4). Divide the fruit filling into three equal portions and roll each portion into a 32 cm (12½ inch) long rope. Divide the pastry into three and, on a lightly floured surface, roll out to 10 x 32 cm (4 x 12½ inch) rectangles.

Brush one length of a rectangle with water. Lay a portion of filling on the strip of pastry near the dry side. Roll the pastry over and press to seal, then cut into eight diagonal pieces and lay, seam side down, on an ungreased baking tray. Repeat with the remaining pastry and filling.

Mix the egg white with 1 tablespoon cold water and glaze the biscuits. Bake for 13–15 minutes, or until golden. Leave to cool on the tray for 2–3 minutes, then transfer to a wire rack.

PREPARATION TIME: 20 MINUTES +   COOKING TIME: 15 MINUTES

CHOCOLATE HAZELNUT SPIRALS

185 g (6½ oz/1½ cups) plain (all-purpose) flour
60 g (2¼ oz/½ cup) unsweetened cocoa powder
115 g (4 oz/½ cup) caster (superfine) sugar
55 g (2 oz/½ cup) ground hazelnuts
100 g (3½ oz) unsalted butter, chopped
1 egg, at room temperature
100 g (3½ oz/⅓ cup) chocolate hazelnut spread, at room temperature

MAKES ABOUT 35

Grease two baking trays and line with baking paper.

Place the flour, cocoa, sugar and ground hazelnuts in a food processor, add the butter and process for 30 seconds, or until the mixture resembles fine crumbs. Add the egg and 1 tablespoon cold water to moisten.

Process until the mixture comes together. Turn the dough onto a lightly floured surface and knead for 30 seconds, or until smooth.

Roll the dough out on a large sheet of baking paper, to form a 25 x 35 cm (10 x 14 inch) rectangle. Trim any uneven edges. Spread the hazelnut spread evenly over the dough.

Using the paper to lift the dough, roll up from the long side to form a log. Wrap tightly in the paper and plastic wrap and refrigerate for 30 minutes. Preheat the oven to 180°C (350°F/Gas 4).

Cut the dough into 1 cm (½ inch) slices. Place on the baking trays, allowing room for spreading. Bake for 10-12 minutes, or until cooked through. Transfer to a wire rack to cool.

PREPARATION TIME: 20 MINUTES +   COOKING TIME: 12 MINUTES

179

LIME AND WHITE CHOCOLATE FINGERS

250 g (9 oz/2 cups) plain (all-purpose) flour
1 teaspoon baking powder
145 g (5 oz/²⁄₃ cup) caster (superfine) sugar
75 g (2½ oz) unsalted butter, melted
2 tablespoons lime juice
grated zest from 2 limes
1 teaspoon vanilla extract
1 egg, at room temperature, lightly beaten
1 egg yolk, at room temperature
150 g (5½ oz/1 cup) chopped white chocolate

MAKES 18

Preheat the oven to 170°C (325°F/Gas 3). Lightly grease and flour two baking trays.

Sift together the flour and baking powder and stir in the sugar. Whisk together the butter, lime juice, zest, vanilla, egg and egg yolk. Add the butter mixture to the flour mixture and stir until a firm dough forms.

Take tablespoonfuls of the dough and, on a lightly floured board, roll into thin logs 12 cm (4½ inches) long. Put on the trays and bake for 10 minutes, or until firm, swapping the position of the trays halfway through cooking. Cool for 5 minutes, then transfer to a wire rack to cool completely.

Put the chocolate in a small heatproof bowl. Sit the bowl over a small saucepan of simmering water, stirring frequently until the chocolate has melted. Don't let the bowl touch the water or the chocolate will get too hot and seize.

To decorate the biscuits, place them close together on the wire rack (put a piece of paper towel under the rack to catch the drips) and, using a fork dipped into the melted chocolate, drizzle the chocolate over the biscuits. Leave to set.

PREPARATION TIME: 20 MINUTES   COOKING TIME: 15 MINUTES

FLORENTINES

55 g (2 oz) unsalted butter
45 g (1½ oz/¼ cup) soft brown sugar
2 teaspoons honey
25 g (1 oz/¼ cup) roughly chopped flaked almonds
2 tablespoons chopped dried apricots
2 tablespoons chopped glacé cherries
2 tablespoons mixed peel
40 g (1½ oz/⅓ cup) plain (all-purpose) flour, sifted
110 g (3¾ oz/¾ cup) dark chocolate

MAKES 12

Preheat the oven to 180°C (350°F/Gas 4). Melt the butter, sugar and honey in a saucepan until the butter has melted and all the ingredients are combined. Remove from the heat and add the almonds, apricots, glacé cherries, mixed peel and the flour. Mix well.

Grease and line two baking trays with baking paper. Place level tablespoons of the mixture on the trays, allowing room for spreading. Reshape and flatten the biscuits into 5 cm (2 inch) rounds before cooking.

Bake for 10 minutes, or until lightly browned. Cool on the trays, then allow to cool completely on a wire rack.

To melt the chocolate, put the chocolate in a heatproof bowl. Half fill a saucepan with water, bring to the boil, then remove from the heat and sit the bowl over the pan (don't let the bowl touch the water or the chocolate will get too hot and seize). Stir occasionally until the chocolate melts.

Spread the melted chocolate on the bottom of each florentine and, using a fork, make a wavy pattern in the chocolate before it sets. Let the chocolate set before serving.

PREPARATION TIME: 15 MINUTES   COOKING TIME: 15 MINUTES

CHOCOLATE PEPPERMINT CREAMS

65 g (2¼ oz) unsalted butter

55 g (2 oz/¼ cup) caster (superfine) sugar

60 g (2¼ oz/½ cup) plain (all-purpose) flour

40 g (1½ oz/⅓ cup) self-raising flour

2 tablespoons unsweetened cocoa powder

2 tablespoons milk

PEPPERMINT CREAM

1 egg white, at room temperature

215 g (7 oz/1¾ cups) icing (confectioners') sugar, sifted

2–3 drops peppermint extract or oil, to taste

CHOCOLATE TOPPING

150 g (5½ oz/1 cup) chopped dark chocolate

150 g (5½ oz/1 cup) dark chocolate melts

MAKES 20

Preheat the oven to 180°C (350°F/Gas 4). Line two baking trays with baking paper.

Cream the butter and sugar with electric beaters until light and fluffy. Add the sifted flours and cocoa alternately with the milk. Mix until the mixture forms a soft dough.

Turn out onto a floured surface and gather into a rough ball. Cut the dough in half. Roll each half between two sheets of baking paper to a 2 mm (⅛ inch) thickness. Slide onto a tray and refrigerate for 15 minutes, or until firm. Cut the dough into rounds using a 4 cm (1½ inch) round cutter, re-rolling the dough scraps and cutting more rounds. Place on the baking trays, allowing room for spreading. Bake for 10 minutes, or until firm. Transfer to a wire rack to cool completely.

To make the peppermint cream, put the egg white in a small bowl. Beat in the icing sugar 2 tablespoons at a time, using electric beaters on low speed. Add more icing sugar, if necessary, until a soft dough forms.

Turn the dough onto a surface dusted with icing sugar and knead in enough icing sugar so that the dough is not sticky. Knead in the peppermint extract.

Roll a teaspoon of peppermint cream into a ball, and flatten slightly. Sandwich between two of the (cooled) chocolate biscuits, pressing together to spread the peppermint to the edges. Repeat with the remaining peppermint cream and chocolate biscuits, keeping the filling covered as you work.

To make the topping, put the chopped chocolate and the chocolate melts in a heatproof bowl. Half fill a saucepan with water and bring to the boil. Remove from the heat and place the bowl over the pan (don't let the bowl touch the water or the chocolate will get too hot and seize). Stir until the chocolate has melted. Allow to cool slightly. Use a fork to dip the biscuits into the chocolate and allow any excess to drain away. Place on a tray lined with baking paper to set.

PREPARATION TIME: 40 MINUTES + COOKING TIME: 15 MINUTES

CHOCOLATE-FILLED SHORTBREADS

125 g (4½ oz) unsalted butter, chopped, softened
60 g (2¼ oz/½ cup) icing (confectioners') sugar
1 teaspoon grated orange zest
125 g (4½ oz/1 cup) self-raising flour
60 g (2¼ oz/½ cup) cornflour (cornstarch)
1 tablespoon icing (confectioners') sugar, extra
1 tablespoon drinking chocolate

FILLING
60 g (2¼ oz/½ cup) roughly chopped dark chocolate
60 g (2¼ oz/¼ cup) cream cheese
1 egg, at room temperature, lightly beaten

MAKES 20

Preheat the oven to 180°C (350°F/Gas 4). Grease and line two baking trays with baking paper.

Using electric beaters, beat the butter, icing sugar and orange rind until light and creamy. Transfer to a food processor and add the sifted flours and 1 tablespoon iced water. Process for 20 seconds or until the mixture comes together. Cover with plastic wrap and refrigerate for 45 minutes.

To make the filling, put the chocolate in a heatproof bowl. Half fill a saucepan with water, bring to the boil, then remove from the heat and sit the bowl over the pan (don't let the bowl touch the water or the chocolate will get too hot and seize). Stir occasionally until the chocolate melts. Remove from the heat. Using electric beaters, beat the cream cheese until soft. Add the cooled chocolate and half the beaten egg. Mix well.

Roll out the shortbread mixture between two sheets of baking paper to a 3 mm (⅛ inch) thickness. Cut into 5 cm (2 inch) rounds using a fluted cutter. Place ½ teaspoon of filling in the centre of half the rounds and brush the edges with the remaining beaten egg. Place the remaining rounds over the filling, and press the edges to seal. Put on the baking trays. Bake for 10–15 minutes, or until golden. Transfer to a wire rack. To serve, dust the shortbreads with sifted icing sugar and chocolate.

PREPARATION TIME: 30 MINUTES +   COOKING TIME: 20 MINUTES

SULTANA AND CHOCOLATE CORNFLAKE COOKIES

60 g (2¼ oz/⅓ cup) dark chocolate bits
60 g (2¼ oz/½ cup) sultanas
30 g (1 oz/¼ cup) roughly chopped walnuts
1 teaspoon grated orange zest
125 g (4½ oz) unsalted butter, chopped
80 g (2¾ oz/⅓ cup) caster (superfine) sugar
1 egg, at room temperature
125 g (4½ oz/1 cup) self-raising flour, sifted
80 g (2¾ oz/2⅔ cups) cornflakes, lightly crushed
80 g (2⅔ oz/½ cup) dark chocolate, melted

MAKES 40

Preheat the oven to 180°C (350°F/Gas 4). Lightly grease two baking trays.

Combine the chocolate bits, sultanas, walnuts and orange zest.

Using electric beaters, beat the butter and sugar until very light and creamy. Add the egg and beat well. Transfer to a large bowl. Using a metal spoon, fold in the flour. Add the sultana mixture and stir well.

Roll 2 level teaspoons of the mixture in the crushed cornflakes to coat. Bake for 15 minutes, or until golden and crisp. Transfer to a wire rack to cool. To serve, drizzle melted chocolate over the cooled cookies.

PREPARATION TIME: 30 MINUTES   COOKING TIME: 15 MINUTES

CHOCOLATE APRICOT COOKIES

125 g (4½ oz) unsalted butter
175 g (6 oz/¾ cup firmly packed) soft brown sugar
1 egg, at room temperature, lightly beaten
30 g (1 oz/¼ cup) unsweetened cocoa powder
90 g (3¼ oz/¾ cup) self-raising flour
60 g (2¼ oz/½ cup) plain (all-purpose) flour
45 g (1¾ oz/¾ cup) shredded coconut
185 g (6 oz/1 cup) chopped dried apricots
270 g (9½ oz/1½ cups) dark chocolate bits

MAKES 40

Preheat the oven to 180°C (350°F/Gas 4). Line two baking trays with baking paper.

Using electric beaters, cream the butter and sugar until light and creamy. Add the egg and beat well. Transfer to a large bowl.

Stir in the sifted cocoa and flours, coconut, apricots and chocolate bits. Mix to a firm dough.

Roll level tablespoons of the mixture into rounds. Put on the trays and flatten slightly. Bake for 15–20 minutes, or until golden. Transfer to a wire rack to cool.

PREPARATION TIME: 15 MINUTES   COOKING TIME: 20 MINUTES

Sultana and chocolate cornflake cookies

CHOCOLATE FUDGE SANDWICHES

250 g (9 oz/2 cups) plain
(all-purpose) flour
30 g (1 oz/$\frac{1}{4}$ cup) unsweetened
cocoa powder
200 g (7 oz) unsalted butter, chilled
and diced
100 g (3$\frac{1}{2}$ oz) icing (confectioners') sugar
2 egg yolks, at room temperature,
lightly beaten
1 teaspoon vanilla extract

FILLING
100 g (3$\frac{1}{2}$ oz/$\frac{2}{3}$ cup) chopped dark
chocolate
1 tablespoon golden syrup or dark
corn syrup
25 g (1 oz) unsalted butter, softened

MAKES 20–24

Preheat the oven to 200°C (400°F/Gas 6). Lightly grease two baking trays.

Sift together the flour and cocoa and rub in the butter until the mixture resembles fine breadcrumbs. Sift in the icing sugar and mix well. Using a wooden spoon, gradually stir in the egg yolks and vanilla until a soft dough forms.

Transfer the dough to a lightly floured work surface and shape into a 4 x 6 x 26 cm (1$\frac{1}{2}$ x 2$\frac{1}{2}$ x 10$\frac{1}{2}$ inch) block. Wrap in plastic wrap and chill for 30 minutes, or until firm. Cut the dough into 40–48 slices, about 5 mm ($\frac{1}{4}$ inch) wide. Place the slices, on the baking trays, allowing room for spreading. Cooking in batches, bake for 10 minutes, or until firm. Cool on the trays for 5 minutes, then transfer to a wire rack to cool completely.

To make the filling, put the chocolate in a small heatproof bowl. Sit the bowl over a saucepan of simmering water. Don't let the bowl touch the water or the chocolate will get too hot and seize. Stir frequently until the chocolate has melted. Remove from the heat, stir in the golden syrup and butter and continue stirring until smooth.

Allow to cool a little, then put in the refrigerator and chill for 10 minutes, or until it becomes a spreadable consistency. Use the chocolate filling to sandwich the biscuits together.

PREPARATION TIME: 20 MINUTES +   COOKING TIME: 30 MINUTES

JAFFA TRIPLE-CHOC BROWNIES

125 g (4½ oz/½ cup) unsalted butter, cubed

350 g (12 oz/2⅓ cups) roughly chopped dark chocolate

185 g (6½ oz/1 cup) soft brown sugar

3 eggs, at room temperature

2 teaspoons grated orange zest

125 g (4½ oz/1 cup) plain (all-purpose) flour

30 g (1 oz/¼ cup) unsweetened cocoa powder

100 g (3½ oz) milk chocolate bits

100 g (3½ oz) white chocolate bits

MAKES 25 PIECES

Preheat the oven to 180°C (350°F/Gas 4). Lightly grease a 23 cm (9 inch) square cake tin and line with baking paper, leaving the paper hanging over on two opposite sides.

Place the butter and 250 g (9 oz/1⅔ cups) of the dark chocolate in a heatproof bowl. Half fill a saucepan with water, bring to the boil, then remove from the heat. Sit the bowl over the saucepan. Stir occasionally until the butter and chocolate have melted. Leave to cool.

Beat together the sugar, eggs and zest until thick and fluffy. Fold in the chocolate.

Sift together the flour and cocoa, then stir into the chocolate mixture. Stir in the remaining dark chocolate and all the chocolate bits. Spread into the tin and bake for 40 minutes, or until just cooked. Cool in the tin before lifting out, using the paper as handles. Cut into squares. To serve, drizzle with melted dark chocolate if desired.

PREPARATION TIME: 20 MINUTES   COOKING TIME: 45 MINUTES

WHITE CHOCOLATE, LEMON AND MACADAMIA BISCOTTI

180 g (6½ oz) unsalted butter, melted
and cooled
230 g (8 oz/1 cup) caster
(superfine) sugar
3 eggs, at room temperature
grated zest from 3 lemons
1 teaspoon vanilla extract
200 g (7 oz/1⅓ cups) chopped white
chocolate
120 g (4¼ oz) macadamia halves
375 g (1 lb/3 cups) plain (all-purpose) flour
1 teaspoon baking powder

MAKES 70

Preheat the oven to 160°C (315°F/Gas 2). Line two baking trays with baking paper.

Whisk together the melted butter, sugar, eggs, lemon zest and vanilla. Stir in the chocolate and macadamias.

Sift together the flour and baking powder. Add to the butter and chocolate mixture and use a wooden spoon to stir to a soft dough (it will be slightly sticky). Divide into four equal portions. On a floured surface, shape each portion into a log about 5 cm (2 inches) wide and 20 cm (8 inches) long. Place on lined trays, allowing room for spreading at least 7 cm (2¾ inches) between each. Slightly flatten each log to about 7 cm (2¾ inches) wide and 24 cm (9½ inches) long.

Bake for 30–35 minutes or the until logs are firm to touch and are just cooked through. Cool on the trays.

Reduce the oven to 150°C (300°F/Gas 2). Use a sharp knife to cut two of the logs diagonally into 1 cm (½ inch) thick slices. Place on a lined baking tray in a single layer. Bake for 20 minutes or until the biscotti are crisp. Cool on the tray, then transfer the biscotti to a wire rack. Repeat with the remaining two logs.

PREPARATION TIME: 20 MINUTES   COOKING TIME: 20 MINUTES

PECAN BROWNIES

125 g (4½ oz) chopped dark chocolate
90 g (3¼ oz) unsalted butter, softened
230 g (8 oz/1 cup) caster (superfine) sugar
1 teaspoon vanilla extract
2 eggs, at room temperature
85 g (3 oz/⅔ cup) plain (all-purpose) flour
30 g (1o oz/¼ cup) unsweetened cocoa powder
½ teaspoon baking powder
125 g (1 cup) roughly chopped pecans

MAKES 16

Preheat the oven to 180°C (350°F/Gas 4). Grease a 17 cm (6¾ inch) square cake tin and line the base with baking paper, hanging it over two opposite sides.

Put the chocolate in a heatproof bowl. Bring a saucepan of water to the boil and remove from the heat. Sit the bowl over the pan. Don't let the bowl touch the water or the chocolate will get too hot and seize. Stand, stirring occasionally, until melted. Cool slightly.

Beat the butter, sugar and vanilla with electric beaters until thick and creamy. Beat in the eggs one at a time, beating well after each addition. Stir in the chocolate.

Fold in the sifted combined flour, cocoa and baking powder with a metal spoon, then fold in the pecans. Spoon into the tin and smooth the surface. Bake for 30-35 minutes, or until firm and the cooked brownie mixture comes away from the sides of the tin. Cool in the tin, then remove and cut into squares and serve.

PREPARATION TIME: 2O MINUTES   COOKING TIME: 4O MINUTES

CHOCOLATE AND GLACE CHERRY SLICE

125 g (4½ oz/1 cup) plain (all-purpose) flour

40 g (1½ oz/⅓ cup) unsweetened cocoa powder

80 g (2¾ oz/⅓ cup) caster (superfine) sugar

125 g (4½ oz) unsalted butter, melted

1 teaspoon vanilla extract

480 g (15 oz/2 cups) finely chopped glacé cherries

60 g (2¼ oz/½ cup) icing (confectioners') sugar

135 g (4¾ oz/1½ cups) desiccated coconut

125 ml (4 fl oz/½ cup) sweetened condensed milk

60 g (2¼ oz) unsalted butter, extra, melted

50 g (1¾ oz) Copha (white vegetable shortening), melted

150 g (5½ oz) dark cooking chocolate

25 g (1 oz) unsalted butter, extra

MAKES 28

Preheat the oven to 180°C (350°F/Gas 4). Lightly grease an 18 x 27 cm (7 x 10½ inch) baking tin and line with baking paper, leaving the paper hanging over the two long sides.

Sift together the flour and cocoa into a bowl, add the sugar, butter and vanilla, then mix to form a dough. Gather together and turn onto a well-floured surface. Press together for 1 minute, then press into the base of the tin. Chill for 20 minutes. Cover with baking paper and baking beads and bake for 10–15 minutes. Remove the paper and beads and bake for a further 5 minutes. Allow to cool to room temperature.

Combine the cherries, icing sugar and coconut. Stir in the condensed milk, extra butter and Copha, then spread over the base. Chill for about 30 minutes.

Chop the chocolate and extra butter into small even-sized pieces and place in a heatproof bowl. Bring a saucepan of water to the boil and remove from the heat. Sit the bowl over the pan. Don't let the bowl touch the water or the chocolate will get too hot and seize. Allow to stand, stirring occasionally, until melted. Pour over the cooled cherry mixture, then chill until set. Cut into squares and serve.

PREPARATION TIME: 25 MINUTES +   COOKING TIME: 25 MINUTES

CHOCOLATE PEANUT SLICE

250 g (9 oz) finely crushed chocolate chip biscuits

130 g (4½ oz) unsalted butter, melted

45 g (1½ oz/¼ cup) soft brown sugar

2 eggs, at room temperature

60 ml (2 fl oz/¼ cup) sweetened condensed milk

250 g (9 oz/1 cup) smooth peanut butter

150 g (5½ oz/1 cup) chopped dark chocolate, melted

2 tablespoons unsweetened cocoa powder

SERVES 8–10

Preheat the oven to 180°C (350°F/Gas 4). Line a 28 x 18 cm rectangular tin with enough baking paper to extend over the longest sides.

Combine the biscuit crumbs and half the melted the butter butter. Press firmly into base of the tin. Refrigerate for 10–15 minutes, or until the mixture is firm.

Using electric beaters, beat the rest of butter and sugar until light and creamy. Add the eggs, condensed milk and peanut butter and mix until smooth. Spread evenly over the biscuit base. Bake for 15–20 minutes, or until lightly golden. Leave in the tin to cool.

Spread the melted chocolate over the cooled slice. Allow the chocolate to set, then remove from the tin. Cut into bars and serve.

PREPARATION TIME: 35 MINUTES   COOKING TIME: 20 MINUTES

COCONUT CHOCOLATE CHERRY TRIANGLES

125 g (4 oz) chopped dark chocolate

3 eggs, at room temperature

170 g (6 oz/¾ cup) caster (superfine) sugar

60 g (2¼ oz) unsalted butter, melted

120 g (3½ oz/½ cup) roughly chopped glacé cherries

225 g (7¼ oz/2½ cups) desiccated coconut

icing (confectioners') sugar, for dusting

MAKES 35

Preheat the oven to 180°C (350°F/Gas 4). Brush a 23 cm (9 inch) square cake tin with melted butter or oil. Line the base with baking paper, allowing the paper to hang over the sides.

Put the chocolate in a heatproof bowl. Half fill a saucepan with water, bring to the boil, then remove from the heat and sit the bowl over the pan (don't let the bowl touch the water or the chocolate will get too hot and seize). Stir occasionally until the chocolate melts. Pour the chocolate into the tin and spread out evenly with the back of a spoon. Allow to set.

Beat the eggs and sugar until pale and creamy, then fold in the butter, cherries and coconut. Pour over the chocolate and smooth the surface. Bake for 15–20 minutes, or until golden. Cool, then refrigerate until set. To serve, remove the paper, cut into triangles and dust with icing sugar.

PREPARATION TIME: 30 MINUTES   COOKING TIME: 25 MINUTES

CHOCOLATE CHEESECAKE SLICE

200 g (7 oz/1½ cups) plain chocolate biscuit crumbs
80 g (2¾ oz) unsalted butter, melted
100 g (3½ oz) chocolate bits

FILLING
375 g (13 oz) cream cheese, softened
115 g (4 oz/½ cup) caster (superfine) sugar
3 eggs, at room temperature
150 g (5½ oz/1 cup) chopped white chocolate, melted

TOPPING
150 g (5½ oz/1 cup) chopped white chocolate, melted
160 g (5¾ oz/⅔ cup) sour cream

SERVES 8–10

Preheat the oven to 180°C (350°F/Gas 4). Grease a 20 x 30 cm rectangular cake tin and line with baking paper, allowing the paper to hang over the longer sides.

Combine the biscuit crumbs and butter. Press into the base of the tin. Sprinkle evenly with the chocolate bits.

To make the filling, use electric beaters to beat the cream cheese until creamy. Beat in the sugar until smooth. Add the eggs one at a time, beating well after each addition. Put the white chocolate in a heatproof bowl. Half fill a saucepan with water, bring to the boil, then remove from the heat and sit the bowl over the pan (don't let the bowl touch the water or the chocolate will get too hot and seize). Stir occasionally until the chocolate melts. Add the chocolate to the cream cheese mixture and beat until smooth. Spread over the base. Bake for 30 minutes, or until just set. Cool, cover and refrigerate until firm.

To make the topping, combine the chocolate and sour cream in a heatproof bowl. Sit the bowl over a pan of simmering water. Stir until the chocolate has melted and the mixture is smooth. Remove from the heat.

Spread evenly over the cheesecake, marking regular lines with a flat-bladed knife. Refrigerate until firm. Cut into slices and serve.

PREPARATION TIME: 40 MINUTES   COOKING TIME: 45 MINUTES

WALNUT AND FIG HEDGEHOG BARS

100 g (3½ oz) broken pieces shredded wheat biscuits
115 g (4 oz/⅔ cup) chopped dried figs
50 g (1¾ oz/½ cup) walnut halves, coarsely chopped
300 g (10½ oz/2 cups) chopped dark chocolate
60 g (2¼ oz) unsalted butter, chopped
90 g (3¼ oz/¼ cup) honey

MAKES 21

Line the base and sides of an 18 cm (7 inch) square cake tin with two strips of baking paper.

Combine the biscuits, figs and walnuts. Combine the chocolate, butter and honey in a small saucepan over low heat. Stir frequently, until the chocolate and butter have melted and the mixture is smooth. Add to the biscuit and fruit mixture and mix well. Spoon evenly into the tin. Tap the tin gently on the bench to settle the mixture.

Cover with plastic wrap and place in the fridge for 1 hour or until firm. Remove from the tin and cut into 2.5 cm x 6 cm (1 x 2½ inch) bars and serve.

PREPARATION TIME: 15 MINUTES   COOKING TIME: 5 MINUTES

CITRUS BLONDIES

200 g (7 oz/1⅓ cups) chopped white chocolate
100 g (3½ oz) unsalted butter
2 eggs, at room temperature
115 g (4 oz/½ cup) caster (superfine) sugar
1½ tablespoons finely grated mandarin zest
2 teaspoons finely grated lime zest
190 g (6¾ oz/1¼ cups) plain (all-purpose) flour
1 teaspoon baking powder
155 g (5½ oz) coarsely chopped white chocolate, extra
100 g (3½ oz/¾ cup) coarsely chopped macadamia nuts, toasted
icing (confectioners') sugar, to dust

MAKES 18

Preheat the oven to 160°C (315°F/Gas 2–3). Line the base and sides of a 20 cm (8 inch) square cake tin with two strips of baking paper.

Combine the chocolate, butter and 2 tablespoons water in a heatproof bowl over a saucepan of simmering water. Stir occasionally until the chocolate and butter just melts and the mixture is smooth. Remove from the heat and set aside until cooled to room temperature.

Use a balloon whisk to whisk the eggs, sugar and mandarin and lime zest into the chocolate. Sift together the flour and baking powder over the chocolate mixture and whisk to combine. Stir in the extra chopped chocolate and macadamias. Pour into the tin and smooth the surface. Bake for 1 hour, or until moist crumbs cling to a skewer when inserted in the centre. Cool in the tin on a wire rack. Cut into bars and serve dusted with icing sugar.

PREPARATION TIME: 15 MINUTES   COOKING TIME: 1 HOUR 5 MINUTES

CHOCOLATE, BLACKBERRY AND COCONUT SLICE

180 g (6 oz/2 cups) desiccated coconut

125 g (10½ oz/2 cups) plain (all-purpose) flour, sifted

165 g (5¾ oz/¾ cup firmly packed) soft brown sugar

200 g (7 oz/1⅓ cups) chopped dark chocolate

100 g (3½ oz) unsalted butter, chopped

2 eggs, at room temperature, lightly beaten

160 g (5½ oz/½ cup) blackberry jam

icing (confectioners') sugar, to dust

MAKES 25

Preheat the oven to 170°C (325°F/Gas 3). Line the base and sides of a 20 cm (8 inch) square cake tin with two strips of baking paper.

Combine the coconut, flour and sugar. Set aside.

Put the chocolate and butter in a small saucepan over low heat, stirring frequently, until the chocolate and butter just melt and the mixture is smooth. Add to the coconut mixture with the eggs and use a wooden spoon to mix well.

Spoon half the chocolate mixture into the tin and press firmly and evenly into the tin. Spread the jam evenly over the chocolate mixture. Top with the remaining mixture, pressing with the back of the spoon to cover the jam and smooth the surface.

Bake for 50 minutes, or until a skewer comes out clean when poked into the centre. Cool in the tin for 10 minutes before using the baking paper to transfer the slice to a wire rack. Cool completely. Cut into 4 cm (1½ inch) squares and serve dusted with icing sugar.

PREPARATION TIME: 15 MINUTES   COOKING TIME: 55 MINUTES

CHOCOLATE CARAMEL SLICE

200 g (7 oz) crushed plain
chocolate biscuits
100 g (3½ oz) unsalted butter, melted
2 tablespoons desiccated coconut
125 g (4½ oz) unsalted butter, extra
400 ml (14 fl oz) tin sweetened
condensed milk
80 g (2¾ oz/⅓ cup) caster (superfine)
sugar
3 tablespoons maple syrup
250 g (9 oz) dark chocolate
2 teaspoons oil

MAKES 24

Grease a 30 x 20 cm (12 x 8 inch) baking tin and line with baking paper, leaving it hanging over the two long sides.

Combine the biscuits, melted butter and coconut, then press into the tin and smooth the surface.

Combine the butter, condensed milk, sugar and maple syrup in a small saucepan. Stir over low heat for 15 minutes, or until the sugar has dissolved and the mixture is smooth, thick and lightly coloured. Remove from the heat and cool slightly. Pour the caramel over the biscuit base and smooth the surface. Refrigerate for 30 minutes, or until firm.

Chop the chocolate into small bite-sized pieces. Put the chocolate in a heatproof bowl. Half fill a saucepan with water, bring to the boil, then remove from the heat and sit the bowl over the pan (don't let the bowl touch the water or the chocolate will get too hot and seize). Allow to stand, stirring occasionally, until the chocolate has melted. Add the oil and stir until smooth. Spread over the caramel and leave until partially set before marking into 24 triangles. Refrigerate until firm. When the slice has set, cut into triangles.

PREPARATION TIME: 15 MINUTES +   COOKING TIME: 20 MINUTES

CHOCOLATE TRUFFLE MACAROON SLICE

3 egg whites, at room temperature
170 g (6 oz/¾ cup) caster (superfine) sugar
180 g (6½ oz/2 cups) desiccated coconut
250 g (9 oz) dark chocolate
300 ml (10½ fl oz/1¼ cups) cream, for whipping
1 tablespoon unsweetened cocoa powder

MAKES 24 PIECES

Preheat the oven to 180°C (350°F/Gas 4). Lightly grease a 20 x 30 cm (8 x 12 inch) baking tin and line with baking paper, leaving it hanging over the two long sides.

Beat the egg whites until soft peaks form. Slowly add the sugar, beating well after each addition until stiff and glossy. Fold in the coconut. Spread into the tin and bake for 20 minutes, or until light brown. While still warm, press down lightly but firmly with a palette knife. Cool completely.

Chop the chocolate into small bite-sized pieces and place in a heatproof bowl. Bring a saucepan of water to the boil, then remove from the heat. Sit the bowl over the pan. Don't let the bowl touch the water or the chocolate will get too hot and seize. Stand, stirring occasionally, until the chocolate has melted. Cool slightly.

Beat the cream until thick. Gently fold in the chocolate — do not overmix or it will curdle. Spread evenly over the base and refrigerate for 3 hours, or until set. Lift from the tin and dust with the cocoa.

PREPARATION TIME: 15 MINUTES   COOKING TIME: 25 MINUTES

MEMORABLE MORSELS

CHEWY CARAMEL AND WALNUT LOGS

125 g (4½ oz) butter, cubed

395 g (14 oz) tin sweetened condensed milk

2 tablespoons golden syrup or light treacle

160 g (5½ oz/¾ cup firmly packed) light brown sugar

100 g (3½ oz/¾ cup) finely chopped walnuts, toasted

250 g (9 oz/1⅔ cups) chopped dark chocolate

MAKES 70

Grease an 18 cm (7 inch) square cake tin and line it with baking paper, leaving it hanging over the two opposite sides for easy removal later.

Combine the butter, condensed milk, golden syrup and sugar in a saucepan over low heat until the butter melts and the sugar dissolves. Increase the heat a little so that the mixture bubbles at a steady slow boil. Stir constantly for 9–10 minutes, or until the mixture is caramel in colour and leaves the side of the pan when stirred. Stir in the walnuts. Pour into the tin and leave at room temperature to cool and set.

Remove from the tin, using the baking paper for handles. Cut into six even pieces. Gently roll each piece into a log approximately 12 cm (4½ inches) long and place on a tray lined with baking paper. Refrigerate for 1 hour, or until firm.

Melt the chocolate in a small bowl over a saucepan of simmering water. Don't let the bowl touch the water or the chocolate will get too hot and seize. Coat each caramel log with the chocolate and put back onto the tray. Return to the fridge until set.

About 10 minutes before serving, take as many logs as you need at the time from the refrigerator. Cut into slices 1–1.5 cm (about ½ inch) thick.

PREPARATION TIME: 20 MINUTES +   COOKING TIME: 20 MINUTES

CHOCOLATE-COATED ORANGE PEEL

2 large thick-skinned oranges
230 g (8 oz/1 cup) caster
(superfine) sugar
150 g (5½ oz/1 cup) chopped
dark chocolate
20 g (¾ oz) Copha (white vegetable
shortening)

MAKES 40

Cut the oranges into quarters. Carefully remove the peel in large sections, removing any excess pith with a sharp knife.

Using a 2 cm (¾ inch) biscuit cutter or a small sharp knife, cut the peel into rounds or shapes. Drop the rounds into a saucepan of boiling water. Simmer for 5 minutes, then drain. Repeat twice more using fresh boiling water each time.

Combine 250 ml (9 fl oz/1 cup) water and the sugar in a saucepan. Stir over low heat, without boiling, until the sugar dissolves. Add the orange rounds and bring to the boil. Reduce the heat and simmer for 5–10 minutes, stirring occasionally, or until the peel is translucent.

Transfer the rounds to a large wire rack to drain. To dry thoroughly, leave the peel to stand overnight, loosely covered with foil.

Combine the chocolate and Copha in a saucepan. Stir over low heat until melted and smooth. Using two forks, half-dip the peel in the chocolate to coat. Drain off any excess chocolate. Stand the rounds on a foil-lined tray until set.

PREPARATION TIME: 30 MINUTES +   COOKING TIME: 35 MINUTES

CHOCOLATE TUILES

1 egg white, at room temperature
60 g (2¼ oz/¼ cup) caster (superfine) sugar
2 tablespoons plain (all-purpose) flour
30 g (1 oz) butter, melted
1 teaspoon vanilla extract
60 g (2 oz) dark chocolate melts, melted

MAKES 12

Preheat the oven to 180°C (350°F/Gas 4). Line two baking trays with baking paper. Draw two 10 cm (4 inch) circles on each sheet of paper.

Combine the egg white, sugar, flour, butter and vanilla until a paste forms. Place the chocolate in a paper piping (icing) bag, seal the end and snip off the tip. Drizzle the chocolate over the baking paper in swirls, following the marked circles. Allow the chocolate to set.

Spread 1½ teaspoons of the egg mixture over the circles. Bake the tuiles, one tray at a time, for 4-6 minutes, or until the edges are just turning golden.

Remove from the oven and quickly shape each circle over a rolling pin. Repeat until you have finished with all of the mixture. Cool the tuiles until crisp.

PREPARATION TIME: 15 MINUTES   COOKING TIME: 35 MINUTES

LAMINGTONS

4 eggs, at room temperature, separated
145 g (5 oz/^{2}/$_3$ cup) caster
(superfine) sugar
2 tablespoons unsweetened cocoa
powder
30 g (1 oz/^{1}/$_4$ cup) plain (all-purpose) flour
30 g (1 oz/^{1}/$_4$ cup) cornflour (cornstarch)
40 g (1^1/$_2$ oz/^{1}/$_3$ cup) self-raising flour

CHOCOLATE ICING
375 g (13 oz/3 cups) icing
(confectioners') sugar
60 g (2^1/$_4$ oz/^{1}/$_2$ cup) unsweetened
cocoa powder
90 g (3^1/$_4$ oz) butter, chopped
1 tablespoon instant coffee powder
270 g (9^1/$_2$ oz/3 cups) desiccated coconut

MAKES 60

Preheat the oven to 180°C (350°F/Gas 4). Line a 20 x 30 cm (8 x 12 inch) cake tin with baking paper.

Using electric beaters, beat the egg whites until soft peaks form. Add the sugar gradually, beating well after each addition. Beat until the sugar dissolves and the mixture is thick and glossy. Add the egg yolks and beat well. Gently fold through the sifted cocoa and flours.

Pour into the tin and smooth the surface. Bake for 20 minutes, or until the cake is springy to the touch. Stand in the tin for 5 minutes before turning out onto a wire rack to cool. Cut into 3 cm (1^1/$_4$ inch) squares.

To make the chocolate icing, sift together the icing sugar and cocoa. Stir in the butter, 185 ml (6 fl oz/^{3}/$_4$ cup) boiling water and the coffee. Mix until smooth. Place the coconut on a large plate. Using two forks, dip the cake squares, one at a time, into the chocolate icing, toss in coconut and then place on a wire rack. Repeat until all the cake squares have been coated. Allow to stand at least 1 hour before serving.

PREPARATION TIME: 40 MINUTES   COOKING TIME: 20 MINUTES

CHOCOLATE MERINGUE KISSES

2 egg whites, at room temperature
115 g (4 oz/½ cup) caster (superfine) sugar
¼ teaspoon ground cinnamon

FILLING
125 g (4½ oz) dark chocolate melts
90 g (3¼ oz/⅓ cup) sour cream

MAKES 25

Preheat the oven to 150°C (300°F/Gas 2). Line 2 baking trays with baking paper.

Using electric beaters, beat the egg whites until soft peaks form. Gradually add the sugar, beating well after each addition. Beat until the sugar has dissolved and the mixture is thick and glossy. Add the cinnamon and beat well.

Transfer to a piping (icing) bag fitted with a 1 cm (½ inch) fluted nozzle. Pipe small stars of 1.5 cm (⅝ inch) diameter onto the trays 3 cm (1¼ inches) apart. Bake for 30 minutes, or until pale and crisp. Turn the oven off and cool with the door ajar.

To make the filling, place the chocolate and sour cream in a small heatproof bowl. Stand the bowl over a saucepan of simmering water. Stir until the chocolate has melted and the mixture is smooth. Remove from the heat and cool slightly.

Sandwich the meringues together with the filling.

PREPARATION TIME: 20 MINUTES   COOKING TIME: 40 MINUTES

EASY CHOCOLATE ORANGE FUDGE

395 g (14 oz) sweetened condensed milk
50 g (1¾ oz) unsalted butter, cubed
200 g (7 oz/1⅓ cups) finely chopped orange-flavoured dark chocolate
200 g (7 oz/1⅓ cups) finely chopped dark chocolate

MAKES 36

Line the base and sides of an 18 cm (7 inch) square cake tin with two strips of baking paper.

Put the condensed milk and butter in a saucepan. Stir over low heat until the butter melts and the mixture is smooth. Bring just to a simmer, stirring frequently. Remove from the heat and set aside for 5 minutes to cool slightly. Add the chocolate and stir until just melted.

Quickly pour the fudge into the tin and smooth the surface. Place in the fridge for 4 hours, or until firm. Remove the fudge from the tin and cut into 3 cm (1¼ inch) squares.

PREPARATION TIME: 10 MINUTES   COOKING TIME: NIL

CHOCOLATE AND ORANGE MARSHMALLOW FUDGE

100 g (3½ oz) pink and white marshmallows
60 ml (2 fl oz/¼ cup) orange juice
90 g (3¼ oz) unsalted butter, cubed
375 g (13 oz/2½ cups) roughly chopped dark chocolate
½ teaspoon vanilla extract
1 teaspoon grated orange zest
185 g (6½ oz) roughly chopped walnuts

CANDIED CITRUS ZEST
1 orange
115 g (4 oz/½ cup) caster (superfine) sugar

MAKES 35

Line the base of a 20 x 30 cm (8 x 12 inch) rectangular cake tin with baking paper, leaving the paper hanging over the two long sides.

Put the marshmallows, orange juice and butter in a saucepan over low heat for 5 minutes. Stir occasionally until the marshmallows have melted. Remove from the heat and cool slightly. Add the chocolate, vanilla, orange zest and walnuts, stirring until the chocolate has melted and the mixture is smooth. Pour into the tin and smooth the surface. Leave to set.

To make the candied citrus zest, remove the rind from the orange and cut into very thin strips. Combine the zest, sugar and 60 ml (2 fl oz/ ¼ cup) water in a saucepan and stir over low heat until the sugar has dissolved. Bring to the boil, then reduce the heat. Simmer, uncovered, for 5 minutes without stirring. Remove the zest from the pan with tongs. Transfer to a wire rack to drain. Cool completely. To serve, cut the fudge into small pieces and top with the candied citrus zest.

PREPARATION TIME: 25 MINUTES   COOKING TIME: 15 MINUTES

CHOCOLATE, GINGER AND NUT PATE

250 g (9 oz/1²/₃ cups) chopped dark chocolate
20 g (³/₄ oz) unsalted butter
160 ml (5¹/₄ fl oz) sweetened condensed milk
2 tablespoons rum or brandy
70 g (2¹/₂ oz/¹/₂ cup) hazelnuts, roasted and skinned
80 g (2³/₄ oz/¹/₂ cup) roasted, unsalted macadamia nuts
50 g (1³/₄ oz/¹/₃ cup) whole almonds, roasted
70 g (2¹/₂ oz/¹/₃ cup) finely chopped glacé (candied) ginger

MAKES 50

Grease a 25 x 8 cm (10 x 3¹/₄ inch) loaf (bar) tin and line it with baking paper. Let the paper hang over the long sides for easy removal later.

Put the chocolate in a heatproof bowl. Half fill a saucepan with water, bring to the boil, then remove from the heat and sit the bowl over the pan (don't let the bowl touch the water or the chocolate will get too hot and seize). Stir frequently, until just melted and smooth. Add the butter, condensed milk and rum or brandy. Stir until smooth.

Remove from the heat, add the nuts and ginger and mix well. Spoon into the tin and smooth the surface. Cover and refrigerate for several hours until firm. Serve chilled, cut into wafer-thin slices.

PREPARATION TIME: 15 MINUTES   COOKING TIME: 5 MINUTES

CHOCOLATE-DIPPED GINGER

250 g (9 oz/1²/₃ cups) chopped dark chocolate
125 g (4¹/₂ oz) crystallised ginger pieces
2 tablespoons unsweetened cocoa powder, to dust
2 tablespoons icing (confectioners') sugar, to dust

MAKES 20

Line a tray with foil. Place half the chocolate in a heatproof bowl over a saucepan of simmering water. Don't let the bowl touch the water or the chocolate will get too hot and seize. Stir occasionally until the chocolate just melts. Remove from the heat.

Dip the crystallised ginger into the chocolate and place on the lined trays. Leave to cool to room temperature until the chocolate is almost set. Use the rest of the chocolate to give the ginger pieces a second coat. When almost set, put the cocoa and icing sugar in separate bowls. Toss half the coated ginger pieces in the cocoa and the other half in the icing sugar. Place the ginger pieces on the tray until the chocolate sets completely.

PREPARATION TIME: 15 MINUTES   COOKING TIME: 5 MINUTES

HONEY AND NUT CHOCOLATE WAFERS

100 g (3½ oz) unsalted butter, cubed
170 g (6 oz/¾ cup) caster (superfine) sugar
60 ml (2 fl oz/¼ cup) runny honey
60 g (2¼ oz/½ cup) plain (all-purpose) flour
2 egg whites, at room temperature
80 g (2¾ oz/½ cup) halved unsalted macadamia nuts
70 g (2½ oz/½ cup) halved roasted, skinned hazelnuts
80 g (2¾ oz/½ cup) roughly chopped dark chocolate

SERVES 12

Preheat the oven to 180°C (350°F/Gas 4). Lightly grease three large baking trays. Cover each with a sheet of baking paper.

In a food processor, process the butter, sugar, honey, flour and egg whites until well blended and smooth.

Using a metal spatula, spread one-third of the mixture evenly and thinly over the entire surface of each baking tray. Or, if the mixture is too difficult to spread, tilt the tray so that it flows evenly over the base.

Scatter each batch with one-third of the combined macadamia nuts, hazelnuts and chocolate.

Bake for 10–12 minutes, or until evenly coloured to a deep golden brown. Cool on the tray until crisp, then break into large pieces.

PREPARATION TIME: 15 MINUTES   COOKING TIME: 12 MINUTES

RUM TRUFFLES

200 g (7 oz/1⅓ cups) finely chopped dark chocolate
60 ml (2 fl oz/¼ cup) cream
30 g (1 oz) unsalted butter
50 g (1¾ oz) chocolate cake crumbs
2 teaspoons dark rum
95 g (3¼ oz/½ cup) chocolate sprinkles

MAKES 25

Line a baking tray with foil.

Place the chocolate in a heatproof bowl. Combine the cream and butter in a saucepan and stir over low heat until the butter melts and mixture is just boiling. Pour the hot cream over the chocolate and stir until the chocolate melts and the mixture is smooth.

Stir in the cake crumbs and rum. Refrigerate for 20 minutes, stirring occasionally, or until firm enough to handle. Roll heaped teaspoons of the mixture into balls.

Spread the chocolate sprinkles on a sheet of baking paper. Roll each truffle in the sprinkles, then place on the tray. Refrigerate for 30 minutes, or until firm. Serve in small paper patty cups, if desired.

PREPARATION TIME: 20 MINUTES +   COOKING TIME: 2 MINUTES

KIRSCH CHOCOLATE CHERRIES

125 g (4½ oz/1 cup) grated dark chocolate
55 g (2 oz/½ cup) ground almonds
1 tablespoon Kirsch
2 tablespoons icing (confectioners') sugar
1 egg white, at room temperature, lightly beaten
25 glacé cherries
30 g (1 oz/¼ cup) unsweetened cocoa powder
30 g (1 oz/¼ cup) drinking chocolate

MAKES 25

Combine the chocolate, ground almonds, Kirsch and icing sugar. Slowly stir in enough egg white to bind the mixture. Refrigerate for about 20 minutes.

Flatten 2 level teaspoons of the mixture in the palm of your hand and work gently to enclose a glacé cherry to create a smooth round ball.

Roll the balls in the combined sifted cocoa and drinking chocolate. Place between layers of baking paper in an airtight container. Refrigerate the balls until hard.

PREPARATION TIME: 20 MINUTES +   COOKING TIME: NIL

LEMON COCONUT TRUFFLES

60 ml (2 fl oz/¼ cup) cream
250 g (9 oz/1⅔ cups) white chocolate
melts
1 tablespoon grated lemon zest
2 teaspoons lemon juice
45 g (1½ oz/½ cup) desiccated coconut
40 g (1½ oz/¾ cup) shredded
coconut, toasted

MAKES 40

Heat the cream and chocolate in a saucepan over low heat until the chocolate just melts. Remove from the heat and stir in the lemon zest, lemon juice and desiccated coconut. Leave to cool for 30 minutes, then refrigerate for 1½ hours.

Roll the mixture into balls and place on a foil-lined tray and refrigerate for 45 minutes. Once set, roll the balls in the shredded coconut.

PREPARATION TIME: 10 MINUTES +   COOKING TIME: 5 MINUTES

EARL GREY-INFUSED CHOCOLATE TRUFFLES

125 ml (4 fl oz/½ cup) thick (double/
heavy) cream
2 tablespoons Earl Grey tea leaves
200 g (7 oz/1⅓ cups) chopped
dark chocolate
20 g (¾ oz) unsalted butter, diced
1 tablespoon icing (confectioners')
sugar, sifted
30 g (1 oz/¼ cup) unsweetened cocoa
powder, for dusting

MAKES 20

Combine the cream and tea leaves in a saucepan and bring to a simmer over medium heat. Remove from the heat, cover and set aside for 30 minutes.

Return the saucepan to low heat and stir until the cream becomes liquid again. Strain the cream through a fine sieve.

Place the strained cream and chocolate in a heatproof bowl over a saucepan of simmering water. Stir frequently until the chocolate just melts and the mixture is smooth. Remove from the heat. Add the butter and icing sugar and stir until the butter melts and the mixture is smooth.

Pour the mixture onto a large plate or tray to form a 20 cm (8 inch) round. Place in the fridge for 1 hour or until firm enough to shape into curls.

Spread the cocoa on a large plate. Use a teaspoon to scrape the chocolate mixture into curls, tossing them in the cocoa as you make them. Transfer the truffles to a serving plate. Sprinkle with any remaining cocoa and return to the fridge for at least 1 hour before serving.

PREPARATION TIME: 20 MINUTES   COOKING TIME: 10 MINUTES

Lemon coconut truffles

WHITE CHOCOLATE AND PISTACHIO MACAROONS

120 g (4¼ oz) whole pistachio kernels
200 g (7 oz/1¼ cups) icing (confectioners')
sugar, sifted
3 egg whites, at room temperature
2 tablespoons caster (superfine) sugar
7 drops green food colouring
icing (confectioners') sugar, to dust

WHITE CHOCOLATE GANACHE
200 g (7 oz/1⅓ cups) finely chopped
white chocolate
60 ml (2 fl oz/¼ cup) cream

MAKES 50

Preheat the oven to 150°C (300°F/Gas 2). Line two large baking trays with baking paper.

Process the pistachios in a food processor until finely ground. Mix with the icing sugar and set aside.

Use electric beaters with a whisk attachment to whisk the egg whites until soft peaks form. Add the caster sugar and whisk until the sugar dissolves. Add the food colouring and whisk until it is combined. Use a large metal spoon to gently fold in the pistachio and icing sugar mixture.

Spoon half the macaroon mixture into a piping (icing) bag fitted with a 1 cm (½ in) nozzle. Pipe 3 cm (1¼ inch) rounds on the trays about 2 cm (¾ inch) apart. Stand at room temperature for 10 minutes, then transfer to the oven and bake for 15 minutes or until the macaroons are crisp on the outside. Turn off the oven and leave the macaroons in the oven to cool with the door ajar.

To make the white chocolate ganache, put the chocolate and cream in a small heatproof bowl over a saucepan of simmering water. Stir frequently until the chocolate just melts and the mixture is smooth. Remove from the heat and put the bowl in the fridge. Stir occasionally until the mixture is a thick, spreadable consistency.

Spread a cooled macaroon with a little white chocolate ganache and sandwich with another macaroon. Repeat with the remaining macaroons and ganache. Serve dusted with icing sugar.

PREPARATION TIME: 20 MINUTES   COOKING TIME: 20 MINUTES

NO-BAKE CHOCOLATE SQUARES

100 g (3¹/₂ oz) roughly crushed
shortbread biscuits
120 g (4¹/₄ oz) pistachio nuts
150 g (5¹/₂ oz/1 cup) hazelnuts, roasted
and skinned
100 g (3¹/₂ oz/¹/₂ cup) glacé (candied)
cherries, roughly chopped
300 g (10¹/₂ oz/2 cups) chopped
dark chocolate
200 g (7 oz) unsalted butter, chopped
1 teaspoon instant coffee granules
2 eggs, at room temperature,
lightly beaten

MAKES 15

Lightly grease an 18 x 27 cm (7 x 10³/₄ inch) baking tin and line with baking paper, leaving the paper hanging over the two long sides. Combine the biscuits, pistachios, 90 g (3¹/₄ oz/²/₃ cup) of the hazelnuts, and half the cherries.

Heat the chocolate and butter in a heatproof bowl over a saucepan of simmering water. Stir occasionally until melted and smooth. Remove from the heat and when cooled slightly, mix in the coffee and eggs.

Pour the chocolate over the biscuit and nut mixture and mix well. Pour into the tin and pat down well. Roughly chop the rest of the hazelnuts and sprinkle them over the top, along with the remaining cherries.

Refrigerate overnight. Remove from the tin and trim the edges before cutting into small pieces.

PREPARATION TIME: 15 MINUTES   COOKING TIME: 5 MINUTES

GLACE FRUIT ROUNDS

80 g (2³/₄ oz/¹/₃ cup) finely chopped
glacé cherries
55 g (2 oz/¹/₄ cup) finely chopped
glacé pineapple
60 g (2¹/₄ oz/¹/₄ cup) finely chopped
glacé apricots
2 tablespoons finely chopped
glacé ginger
1 tablespoon brandy
185 g (6¹/₂ oz/1¹/₄ cups) roughly chopped
milk chocolate

MAKES 70

Line a baking tray with baking paper. Combine the glacé fruit and brandy. Leave to stand for 2 hours.

Put the chocolate in a heatproof bowl. Half fill a saucepan with water, bring to the boil, then remove from the heat and sit the bowl over the pan (don't let the bowl touch the water or the chocolate will get too hot and seize). Stir occasionally until the chocolate melts.

Place ¹/₂ teaspoons of melted chocolate on the tray and shape into circles. Quickly put ¹/₄ teaspoon of the fruit mixture on top of each circle and press gently.

Put in the fridge and allow to set. Remove the rounds gently from the paper using a flat knife.

PREPARATION TIME: 25 MINUTES   COOKING TIME: 5 MINUTES

No-bake chocolate squares

237

FRECKLES

150 g (5½ oz/1 cup) milk chocolate melts
sprinkles of your choice (such as 100s
and 1,000s, silver or mixed cachous
and/or coloured sprinkles)

MAKES 12

Line a large tray with baking paper.

Put the chocolate in a heatproof bowl. Half fill a saucepan with water, bring to the boil, then remove from the heat and sit the bowl over the pan (don't let the bowl touch the water or the chocolate will get too hot and seize). Stir occasionally until the chocolate just melts. Remove from the heat.

Spoon 2 teaspoon measures of the chocolate onto the lined tray, spacing them about about 5 cm (2 inches) apart to form about 12 rounds. Tap the tray on the bench lightly to spread the chocolate out to form 5 cm (2 inch) discs. Sprinkle the chocolate discs with sprinkles of your choice. Set aside at room temperature for 30 minutes, or until set.

PREPARATION TIME: 10 MINUTES   COOKING TIME: 5 MINUTES

CHOCOLATE CRACKLES

75 g (2½ oz/2½ cups) rice bubbles
90 g (3¼ oz/1 cup) desiccated coconut
250 g (9 oz/1²/₃ cups) chopped
dark chocolate
icing (confectioners') sugar, to dust

MAKES 36

Line three 12-hole mini muffin trays with paper cases.

Combine the rice bubbles and coconut. Put the chocolate in a heatproof bowl over a saucepan of simmering water. Don't let the bowl touch the water or the chocolate will get too hot and seize. Stir occasionally until the chocolate just melts. Remove from the heat.

Add the melted chocolate to the rice bubble mixture and use a wooden spoon to stir gently, mixing well. Divide the mixture evenly among the paper cases. Put in the fridge for 1 hour, or until set. Dust with icing sugar before serving.

PREPARATION TIME: 10 MINUTES   COOKING TIME: NIL

CHOCOLATE SWIRL ALMOND NOUGAT

4 sheets rice paper 5.5 cm x 23.5 cm
(6 x 9 inches) each
150 g (5½ oz/1 cup) chopped
dark chocolate
550 g (1 lb 4 oz/2½ cups) caster
(superfine) sugar
330 ml (11¼ fl oz/1⅓ cups) liquid glucose
115 g (4 oz/⅓ cup) honey
2 egg whites, at room temperature
155 g (5½ oz/1 cup) whole blanched
almonds, toasted

MAKES 40

Line the base and two long sides of a 16 x 26 cm (6¼ x 10½ inch) cake tin with one piece of baking paper, allowing it to hang over the sides. Cover the base of the tin with two sheets of the rice paper so that they are slightly overlapping.

Put the chocolate in a small heatproof bowl over a saucepan of simmering water. Don't let the bowl touch the water or the chocolate will get too hot and seize. Stir occasionally until the chocolate just melts. Remove from the heat.

Put the sugar, liquid glucose and honey in a saucepan. Stir over low heat until the sugar dissolves, frequently brushing down the side of the pan with a pastry brush dipped in water. Increase the heat to high and bring to the boil. Place a sugar thermometer in the syrup and boil, uncovered, without stirring, frequently brushing down the side of the pan with the brush, until the syrup reaches 140°C (284°F).

Use an electric beater with a whisk attachment to whisk the egg whites until stiff peaks form. Remove the syrup from the heat and allow the bubbles to subside. On medium speed, add the syrup to the egg whites in a thin steady stream until the mixture is very thick and glossy. Immediately add the melted chocolate and almonds and use a large metal spoon to fold together to form a swirl pattern (don't take too long as the mixture will start to set).

Pour into the tin. Place the two remaining pieces of rice paper on top of the nougat to cover, cutting to fit, and press down firmly to smooth the surface. Set aside in a cool, dry place for 6 hours, or until set.

Transfer the nougat to a cutting board and cut into 2 x 5 cm (¾ x 2 inch) pieces.

PREPARATION TIME: 20 MINUTES   COOKING TIME: 20 MINUTES

RUM AND RAISIN CLUSTERS

100 g (3½ oz/¾ cup) raisins
1 tablespoon Malibu (coconut and
rum liqueur)
50 g (1¾ oz/¾ cup) shredded coconut
400 g (14 oz/2⅔ cups) chopped
dark chocolate
100 g (3½ oz/⅔ cup) pine nuts, roasted

MAKES 32

Put the raisins and Malibu in a bowl, cover and leave overnight.

Preheat the oven to 150°C (300°F/Gas 2). Spread the coconut on a baking tray and bake for 5–10 minutes, or until lightly golden. Remove from the oven, lift the baking paper and coconut off the tray and set aside to cool. Line the baking tray with fresh baking paper. Put the chocolate in a heatproof bowl. Half fill a saucepan with water, bring to the boil, then remove from the heat and sit the bowl over the pan (don't let the bowl touch the water or the chocolate will get too hot and seize). Stir frequently until the chocolate has melted and is smooth.

Drain the raisins well. Remove the chocolate from the heat and stir in the raisins, coconut and pine nuts. Using oiled teaspoons, take spoonfuls of mixture and shape into loose balls. Don't squash them too firmly, but just enough for them to cling together, with bits of coconut and pine nuts sticking out. Put onto the prepared tray. Leave to dry, then refrigerate until set completely.

PREPARATION TIME: 15 MINUTES +   COOKING TIME: 15 MINUTES

WHITE CHOCOLATE BARK

150 g (5½ oz/1 cup) unsalted macadamia
nuts, chopped
250 g (9 oz/1⅔ cups) chopped
white chocolate
120 g (4¼ oz/⅔ cup) finely chopped
dried apricots
50 g (1¾ oz/⅓ cup) currants

SERVES 8–10

Preheat the oven to 180°C (350°F/Gas 4) and line a baking tray with baking paper. Spread the nuts over a second baking tray. Roast for 5–6 minutes, or until lightly browned, shaking the tray once or twice to ensure even roasting. Leave to cool.

Put the chocolate in a heatproof bowl. Half fill a saucepan with water, bring to the boil, then remove from the heat and sit the bowl over the pan (don't let the bowl touch the water or the chocolate will get too hot and seize). Remove from the heat. Add two-thirds of the nuts and dried fruit and stir to coat.

Pour onto the lined tray and spread to a square of approximately 25 cm (10 inches). Scatter over the remaining nuts and fruit. Cover with plastic wrap and refrigerate until set. Break into large chunks and serve.

PREPARATION TIME: 15 MINUTES   COOKING TIME: 10 MINUTES

CHERRY AND ALMOND CHOCOLATE BARK

200 g (7 oz/1⅓ cups) chopped
dark chocolate
70 g (2½ oz/⅓ cup) dried cherries
40 g (1½ oz/⅓ cup) slivered almonds

MAKES 25

Line a baking tray with baking paper.

Put the chocolate in a heatproof bowl. Half fill a saucepan with water, bring to the boil, then remove from the heat and sit the bowl over the pan (don't let the bowl touch the water or the chocolate will get too hot and seize). Stir occasionally until the chocolate just melts. Remove from the heat.

Pour the chocolate onto the tray and spread evenly into a 20 cm (8 inch) square. Tap the tray on the bench to settle the chocolate. Sprinkle with the cherries and almonds. Set aside in a cool place for 3–4 hours or until the chocolate has set.

Break the chocolate bark into rough 4 cm (1½ inch) pieces and serve.

PREPARATION TIME: 10 MINUTES   COOKING TIME: 5 MINUTES

White chocolate bark

ROCKY ROAD

250 g (9 oz/2¾ cups) pink and white marshmallows, halved
160 g (5½ oz/1 cup) roughly chopped unsalted peanuts
100 g (3½ oz/½ cup) glacé (candied) cherries, halved
60 g (2¼ oz/1 cup) shredded coconut
350 g (12 oz/2⅓ cups) chopped dark chocolate

MAKES 30 PIECES

Line the base and two opposite sides of a 20 cm (8 inch) square cake tin with foil.

Combine the marshmallows, peanuts, cherries and coconut. Put the chocolate in a heatproof bowl and set over a saucepan of simmering water. Don't let the bowl touch the water, or the chocolate will get too hot and seize. Stir occasionally until just melted and smooth. Add the chocolate to the marshmallow mixture and toss together.

Spoon into the tin and press evenly over the base. Refrigerate for several hours, or until set. Carefully lift the rocky road out of the tin, then peel away the foil and cut it into small pieces.

PREPARATION TIME: 15 MINUTES   COOKING TIME: 5 MINUTES

CHOCOLATE ALMOND TOFFEE

90 g (3¼ oz/1 cup) flaked almonds, roasted
145 g (5 oz/⅔ cup) caster (superfine) sugar
150 g (5½ oz/1 cup) dark chocolate melts

MAKES 25

Line a flat or baking tray with baking paper. Spread the almonds over the tray.

Combine the sugar and 125 ml (2 fl oz/½ cup) water in a saucepan. Stir over low heat without boiling, until the sugar dissolves, brushing down the side of the pan with a pastry brush dipped in water to remove the sugar crystals. Bring the mixture to the boil, then reduce the heat and simmer for 10–15 minutes, or until the mixture turns a golden colour. Work quickly and pour the toffee over the almonds. Allow to set. When set, cut the toffee into thin small wedges or break into pieces.

Put the chocolate in a heatproof bowl. Half fill a saucepan with water, bring to the boil, then remove from the heat and sit the bowl over the pan (don't let the bowl touch the water or the chocolate will get too hot and seize).

Remove from the heat. Dip the wide end of the toffee pieces into the chocolate. Allow to set on a foil-lined tray.

PREPARATION TIME: 15 MINUTES   COOKING TIME: 20 MINUTES

PRALINE LIQUEUR-FILLED CHOCOLATE DATES

PRALINE FILLING
50 g (1¾ oz/⅓ cup) chopped dark chocolate
30 g (1 oz) unsalted butter, softened
2 tablespoons finely chopped vienna almonds
1 tablespoon Grand Marnier or other orange liqueur
15 dates
50 g (1¾ oz/⅓ cup) chopped milk chocolate

MAKES 15

To make the praline filling, put the chocolate in a heatproof bowl. Half fill a saucepan with water, bring to the boil, then remove from the heat and sit the bowl over the pan (don't let the bowl touch the water or the chocolate will get too hot and seize). Stir occasionally until the chocolate melts. Remove from the heat and set aside to cool.

Beat the butter until pale and creamy. Whisk in the melted chocolate, then add the ground almonds and Grand Marnier. Cover and refrigerate until firm but not hard.

Use a small, sharp knife to make a slit along each date and remove the stone. Put the praline filling in a piping (icing) bag and fill the dates with the filling. Smooth off the filling along the cut edge with a small knife. Refrigerate on a tray.

Put the chocolate in a heatproof bowl and stand over a saucepan of simmering water, stirring frequently, until just melted and smooth. (don't let the bowl touch the water, or the chocolate will get too hot and seize). Remove from the heat. Put the chocolate in a piping (icing) bag and squiggle the chocolate across the dates in a decorative fashion.

Cover and refrigerate to firm the filling and to set the chocolate. Serve chilled.

PREPARATION TIME: 20 MINUTES +   COOKING TIME: 10 MINUTES

INDEX

INDEX

angel food cake with chocolate
  sauce 11
apricot, chocolate apricot cookies 189

banana
  banana cream pie 81
  chocolate banana cake 23
bavarois, chocolate 113
beetroot, chocolate beetroot cakes 47
berries
  cheesecakes with mixed berries 70
  chocolate, blackberry and coconut
    slice 206
  chocolate and chestnut marquis
    loaf 126
  chocolate swirl pavlova with
    dipped strawberries 121
  devil's food cake with strawberry
    cream 27
  raspberry and white chocolate
    roll 101
  white chocolate and coconut
    semifreddo with blackberries
    97
  white chocolate and raspberry
    ripple rice pudding 137
biscuits
  chocolate fudge sandwiches 190
  chocolate hazelnut spirals 178
  chocolate peppermint creams 185
  chocolate-filled shortbreads 186
  dried fruit and chocolate pillows
    177
  Florentines 182
  freckles 239
  lime and white chocolate fingers
    181
  white chocolate, lemon and
    macadamia biscotti 194

white chocolate and pistachio
  macaroons 235
  see also cookies
Black Forest cake 24
black and white chocolate tart 54
bread, chocolate 85
brownies
  jaffa triple-choc brownies 193
  pecan brownies 197
butterfly cakes 38

cakes
  angel food cake with chocolate
    sauce 11
  Black Forest cake 24
  chocolate and almond refrigerator
    cake 31
  chocolate banana cake 23
  chocolate chestnut roulade 35
  chocolate mousse meringue
    cake 20
  chocolate rum and raisin cake 40
  chocolate walnut ring 19
  date chocolate torte 19
  devil's food cake with strawberry
    cream 27
  flourless chocolate cake 12
  marble cake 16
  orange, lemon and white chocolate
    gateau 43
  rich chocolate and whisky mud
    cake with sugared violets 48
  rich fudge and marshmallow
    crust cake 16
  Sacher torte 36
  Yule log 32
cakes, small
  butterfly cakes 38
  chocolate beetroot cakes 47
  chocolate muffins 23
  ginger cakes with chocolate
    centres 44
  lamingtons 220

white chocolate and almond
  cakes 15
caramel
  caramel tarts with chocolate
    ganache 89
  chewy caramel and walnut logs 215
  chocolate caramel slice 209
  chocolate crème caramel 117
  cheese, coffee crémets with
    chocolate sauce 118
cheesecake
  baked chocolate cheesecake 77
  cheesecakes with mixed berries 70
  chocolate cheesecake slice 202
cherries
  cherry and almond chocolate
    bark 244
  chocolate cherry trifle 105
  chocolate and glacé cherry
    slice 198
  coconut chocolate cherry
    triangles 201
  Kirsch chocolate cherries 231
chestnut
  chocolate and chestnut marquis
    loaf 126
  chocolate chestnut roulade 35
chocolate 7
  baked chocolate cheesecake 77
  baked chocolate custards 98
  chocolate affogato 109
  chocolate and almond refrigerator
    cake 31
  chocolate almond toffee 247
  chocolate apricot cookies 189
  chocolate banana cake 23
  chocolate bavarois 113
  chocolate beetroot cakes 47
  chocolate, blackberry and
    coconut slice 206
  chocolate bread 85
  chocolate bread and butter
    pudding 133

chocolate caramel slice 209
chocolate cheesecake slice 202
chocolate cherry trifle 105
chocolate and chestnut marquis
    loaf 126
chocolate chestnut roulade 35
chocolate chip cookies 173
chocolate chip pancakes with
    hot fudge sauce 165
chocolate and cinnamon
    self-saucing puddings 157
chocolate crackles 239
chocolate crème caramel 117
chocolate crepes with Grand
    Marnier sauce 150
chocolate croissant pudding 138
chocolate éclairs 53
chocolate French toast 149
chocolate fudge pecan pie 57
chocolate fudge pudding 142
chocolate fudge sandwiches 190
chocolate and glacè cherry
    slice 198
chocolate hazelnut spirals 178
chocolate honeycomb pastries 86
chocolate liqueur frappé 109
chocolate Malakoff 114
chocolate meringue kisses 223
chocolate meringue tower 129
chocolate mint self-saucing
    pudding 158
chocolate mousse flan 82
chocolate mousse meringue
    cake 20
chocolate muffins 23
chocolate, ginger and nut pâté 227
chocolate and orange marshmallow
    fudge 224
chocolate orange tarts 69
chocolate and peanut butter pie 78
chocolate peanut slice 201
chocolate peppermint creams 185
chocolate raisin scrolls 73

chocolate ravioli 134
chocolate ricotta tart 66
chocolate rum fondue 166
chocolate rum and raisin cake 40
chocolate sauce 65
chocolate soufflé 154
chocolate swirl almond nougat 240
chocolate swirl pavlova with
    dipped strawberries 121
chocolate tartufo 125
chocolate truffle macaroon slice
    210
chocolate tuiles 219
chocolate walnut ring 19
petits pots au chocolate 106
three chocolates tart 74
chocolate-coated orange peel 217
chocolate-filled shortbreads 186
chunky monkey sundae 94
cinnamon, chocolate and cinnamon
    self-saucing puddings 157
citrus blondies 205
cocoa and date crostata 58
coconut
    chocolate, blackberry and
        coconut slice 206
    chocolate crackles 239
    chocolate truffle macaroon
        slice 210
    coconut chocolate cherry
        triangles 201
    lemon coconut truffles 232
    white chocolate and coconut
        semifreddo with
        blackberries 97
coffee
    chocolate affogato 109
    chocolate Malakoff 114
    coffee crèmets with chocolate
        sauce 118
    dark chocolate puddings with rich
        coffee liqueur mocha sauce 162
    hot mocha soufflé 141

    mocha coffee cream pots 102
    profiteroles with coffee
        mascarpone and dark
        chocolate sauce 65
cookies
    chocolate apricot cookies 189
    chocolate chip cookies 173
    crackle cookies 174
    sultana and chocolate cornflake
        cookies 189
    tollhouse cookies 174
see also biscuits
cornflakes, sultana and chocolate
    cornflake cookies 189
crackle cookies 174
crème caramel, chocolate 117
crepes
    chocolate chip pancakes with
        hot fudge sauce 165
    chocolate crepes with Grand
        Marnier sauce 150
custard
    baked chocolate custards 98
    chocolate crème caramel 117

dark chocolate puddings with
    rich coffee liqueur mocha
    sauce 162
dates
    cocoa and date crostata 58
    date chocolate torte 19
    praline liqueur-filled chocolate
        dates 248
desserts
    chocolate crepes with Grand
        Marnier sauce 150
    chocolate soufflé 154
    hot mocha soufflé 141
    pears in spiced chocolate syrup
        146
    waffles with hot chocolate
        sauce 158
    see also puddings

devil's food cake with strawberry
cream 27
drinks
chocolate liqueur frappé 109
cocoa-scented tea 169
the ultimate hot chocolate 169

Earl Grey-infused chocolate truffles
232
éclairs, chocolate 53

figs, walnut and fig hedgehog bars
205
flan, chocolate mousse 82
Florentines 182
flourless chocolate cake 12
fondue
chocolate rum fondue 166
white chocolate fondue with
fruit 166
freckles 239
French toast, chocolate 149
fruit
dried fruit and chocolate
pillows 177
glacé fruit rounds 236
fudge
chocolate chip pancakes with
hot fudge sauce 165
chocolate fudge pecan pie 57
chocolate fudge pudding 142
chocolate fudge sandwiches 190
chocolate and orange marshmallow
fudge 224
chunky monkey sundae 94
easy chocolate orange fudge 224

gelato
chocolate affogato 109
chocolate tartufo 125
ginger
chocolate, ginger and nut pâté 227
chocolate-dipped ginger 227

ginger cakes with chocolate
centres 44
glaé fruit rounds 236

hazelnuts, chocolate hazelnut
spirals 178
honey
honey and nut chocolate wafers
228
Masala and honey chocolate
sorbet 102
honeycomb, chocolate honeycomb
pastries 86
hot chocolate, the ultimate 169
hot mocha soufflé 141

jaffa triple-choc brownies 193

Kahlùa chocolate parfait 93
Kirsch chocolate cherries 231

lamingtons 220
lemon coconut truffles 232
lime and white chocolate fingers 181
liqueur
chocolate crepes with Grand
Marnier sauce 150
chocolate liqueur frappé 109
chocolate Malakoff 114
chocolate swirl pavlova with
dipped strawberries 121
dark chocolate puddings with rich
coffee liqueur mocha sauce 162
pannacotta with poached raisins
110
praline liqueur-filled chocolate
dates 248
steamed chocolate and prune
puddings 145
white chocolate fondue with
fruit 166
zuccotto 122
see also rum

macadamia, white chocolate, lemon
and macadamia biscotti 194
marble cake 16
marshmallow
chocolate and orange marshmallow
fudge 224
chunky monkey sundae 94
Masala and honey chocolate sorbet
102
meringue
chocolate meringue kisses 223
chocolate meringue tower 129
chocolate mousse meringue
cake 20
chocolate swirl pavlova with
dipped strawberries 121
raspberry and white chocolate
roll 101
mocha coffee cream pots 102
mousse
chocolate mousse flan 82
rum chocolate mousse 93
muffins, chocolate 23

nougat, chocolate swirl almond 240

orange
chocolate and orange marshmallow
fudge 224
chocolate orange tarts 69
chocolate-coated orange peel 217
easy chocolate orange fudge 224
jaffa triple-choc brownies 193
orange, lemon and white chocolate
gateau 43

pannacotta with poached raisins
110
parfait, Kahlùa chocolate 93
pâté, chocolate, ginger and nut 227
peanuts
chocolate and peanut butter pie 78
chocolate peanut slice 201

pears
    individual chocolate and almond
        pear puddings 161
    pears in spiced chocolate
        syrup 146
pecans
    chocolate fudge pecan pie 57
    pecan brownies 197
peppermint
    chocolate mint self-saucing
        pudding 158
    chocolate peppermint creams 185
petits pots au chocolate 106
pies
    banana cream pie 81
    chocolate fudge pecan pie 57
    chocolate and peanut butter pie 78
pistachio, white chocolate and
    pistachio macaroons 235
praline liqueur-filled chocolate dates 248
profiteroles with coffee mascarpone
    and dark chocolate sauce 65
prunes, steamed chocolate and prune
    puddings 145
puddings
    chocolate bread and butter
        pudding 133
    chocolate and cinnamon
        self-saucing puddings 157
    chocolate croissant pudding 138
    chocolate fudge pudding 142
    chocolate mint self-saucing
        pudding 158
    dark chocolate puddings with rich
        coffee liqueur mocha sauce 162
    individual chocolate and almond
        pear puddings 161
    molten chocolate puddings 153
    steamed chocolate and prune
        puddings 145
    white chocolate and raspberry
        ripple rice pudding 137
    zuccotto 122

raisins
    chocolate raisin scrolls 73
    panna cotta with poached raisins
        110
    rum and raisin bagatelles 243
raspberry and white chocolate roll 101
ravioli, chocolate 134
rice pudding, white chocolate and
    raspberry ripple 137
rich chocolate and whisky mud cake
    with sugared violets 48
rich fudge and marshamallow crust
    cake 16
ricotta
    chocolate ricotta tart 66
    Sicilian cannoli 61
rocky road 247
rum
    chocolate rum fondue 166
    chocolate rum and raisin cake 40
    rum chocolate mousse 93
    rum and raisin bagatelles 243
    rum truffles 231

Sacher torte 36
semifreddo, white chocolate and
    coconut, with blackberries 97
Sicilian cannoli 61
slices
    chocolate, blackberry and coconut
        slice 206
    chocolate caramel slice 209
    chocolate cheesecake slice 202
    chocolate and glacé cherry
        slice 198
    chocolate peanut slice 201
    chocolate truffle macaroon
        slice 210
    citrus blondies 205
    coconut chocolate cherry
        triangles 201
    no-bake chocolate squares 236
    walnut and fig hedgehog bars 205

sorbet, Marsala and honey
    chocolate 102
soufflés
    chocolate soufflé 154
    hot mocha soufflé 141
sultana and chocolate cornflake
    cookies 189
sundae, chunky monkey 94
sweets
    Earl Grey-infused chocolate
        truffles 232
    Kirsch chocolate cherries 231
    lemon coconut truffles 232
    rum truffles 231

tarts
    black and white chocolate
        tart 54
    caramel tarts with chocolate
        ganache 89
    chocolate tart 62
    chocolate orange tarts 69
    chocolate ricotta tart 66
    cocoa and date crostata 58
    three chocolates tart 74
tartufo, chocolate 125
tea, cocoa-scented 169
toffee, chocolate almond 247
tollhouse cookies 174
torte
    Sacher torte 36
    wicked walnut and chocolate
        plum torte 28
trifle, chocolate cherry 105
truffles
    Earl Grey-infused chocolate
        truffles 232
    lemon coconut truffles 232
    rum truffles 231
tuiles, chocolate 219

violets, sugared 48
wafers, honey and nut chocolate 228

waffles with hot chocolate sauce 158
walnuts
    chewy caramel and walnut logs 215
    chocolate walnut ring 19
    walnut and fig hedgehog bars 205
    wicked walnut and chocolate
        plum torte 28
whisky, rich chocolate and whisky mud
    cake with sugared violets 48
white chocolate
    citrus blondies 205
    lime and white chocolate fingers
        181
    orange, lemon and white chocolate
        gateau 43
    raspberry and white chocolate
        roll 101
    white chocolate and almond
        cakes 15
    white chocolate bark 244
    white chocolate and coconut
        semifreddo with blackberries
        97
    white chocolate fondue with
        fruit 166
    white chocolate, lemon and
        macadamia biscotti 194
    white chocolate and pistachio
        macaroons 235
    white chocolate and raspberry
        ripple rice pudding 137

Yule log 32

zuccotto 122